Improvised
LOCK PICKING

To Craig "T" Herrington.
You motivate with your curiosity, humor, and wit.

Secrets from
the Master

Steven Hampton

Improvised
LOCK PICKING

PALADIN PRESS • BOULDER, COLORADO

Other books by Steven Hampton

Advanced Lock Picking Secrets
Affordable Security
Modern High-Security Locks
Secrets of Lockpicking

Improvised Lock Picking: Secrets from the Master
by Steven Hampton

Copyright © 2003 by Steven Hampton

ISBN 13: 978-1-58160-396-5
Printed in the United States of America

Published by Paladin Press, a division of
Paladin Enterprises
Gunbarrel Tech Center
7077 Winchester Circle
Boulder, Colorado 80301 USA
+1.303.443.7250

Direct inquiries and/or orders to the above address.

Visit our Web site at www.paladin-press.com

Drawings by Steven Hampton
Photographs by Delores Hampton

TABLE OF CONTENTS

WARNING

INTRODUCTION

A lock is a puzzle. The solution to the puzzle is its key. So each lock is like a complex question, and the key is its simple answer. But a complex question has more than one simple answer: if there is a keyhole or access port, the lock can be opened by means other than the original key or code. Cracking codes, for that matter—whether they are a simple safe lock or a complex computer program—requires imagination to see beyond the obvious. In the same way, if we look around us, we find the tools we need to crack the code of any lock . With the information in this book, you'll learn how to open any kind of lock found anywhere in the world with improvised tools made from common objects found in the home, office, or garage.

Chapter 1
INVISIBLE LOCK PICKS

Finding the right tool for any job is a universal problem. However, tools needed to pick most locks are all around us. The agent must think like MacGyver (the lead character on the *MacGyver* television show that ran from 1985 to 1991) when it comes to survival. Magical Swiss Army knife aside, the lighter one can travel, the better his chances of accomplishing the task at hand.

MATERIALS USED IN THIS BOOK

All lockpicking items can be found at home and in most foreign countries and can be abandoned with little effort or without arousing suspicion. Here is a list of those items you'll need for practice here at home:

1. 1 standard nut pick
2. 6-inch piece of 1/4-inch-diameter copper tubing
3. 12 large paper clips (could be attached to papers)
4. 12 small paper clips (could be attached to papers)
5. 1 bobby pin (attached to hair)
6. 1 coat hanger, thin wire .065- to .073-inch diameter
7. 1 small flat-blade pocket screwdriver
8. 1 medium flat-blade screwdriver (1/4-inch blade)
9. 4 safety pins (2 each, #2 and #3)
10. 1 small vise
12. 1 small hammer
13. 1 disposable lighter
14. 1 small can of 3-in-1 household oil
15. 1 file (optional)
16. 1 pocket penlight (best from the country you are in)
17. 1 hacksaw blade
18. 1 roll masking tape
19. 1 bottle rubbing alcohol
20. 1 roll paper towels

These tools are covered in more detail as specific locks are discussed; most tools need to be custom-fitted to the particular lock you want to pick, and this will make it easier for you to make them. However, the most versatile homemade tools needed for all *cylinder* locks in worldwide use today are the safety-pin "hook" pick and the small-screwdriver "tension wrench."

NOTE: Read the entire chapter before attempting to make tools.

Figure 1 (page 4) displays the improvised or homemade lock picks used on nearly all the locks in this book. They are drawn as close to exact scale as possible with the inside line being the true dimension. Let's look briefly at each tool.

1. Safety pin "hook" pick, #3 (about 2 inches long closed). Employed in Chapter 3, it is used on all pin- and wafer-tumbler house, car, and cabinet locks, including padlocks and modern suitcase locks. It can be used on small lever padlocks and older suitcases as well.

2. Pocket screwdriver "tension wrench." Also employed in Chapter 3, this tool is used in conjunction with the safety-pin hook pick on all pin- and wafer-tumbler house, car, and cabinet locks, including most padlocks.

1. Safety pin, #3, "hook" pick
2. Pocket screwdriver
3. Nut pick
4. Safety pin, #2
5. Small paper clip
6. Large paper clip L pick
7. Large paper clip
8. Bobby pin
9. Coat hanger wire T pick
10. Copper-tube pick, 1/4-inch outer diameter (OD)

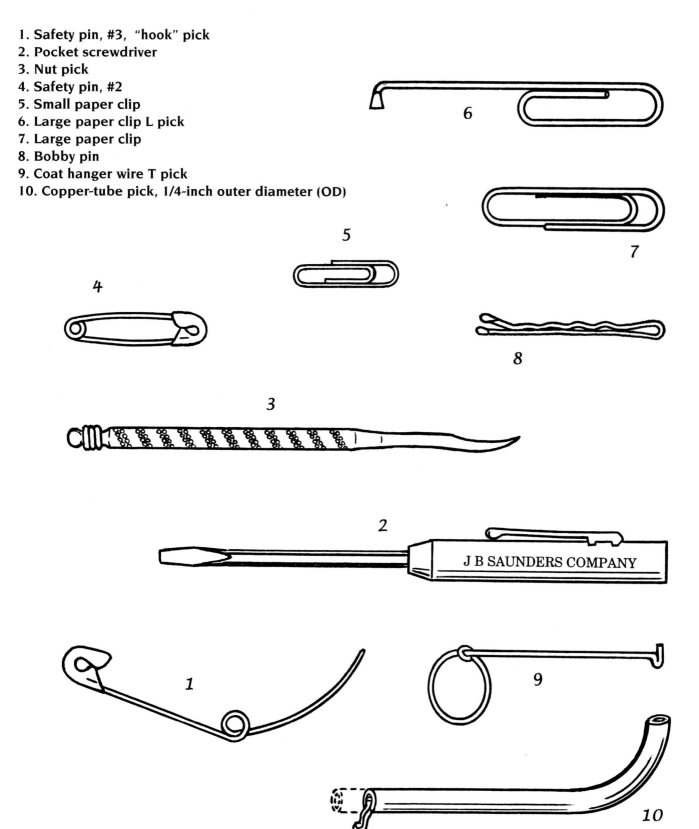

FIGURE 1

3. Nut pick. The standard, garden-variety munchie tool is used to pry the delectable meat from the shell. Most people nowadays buy bags of shelled nuts, so the classic Christmas gift of a nutcracker-and-pick set can be found filed under "unused gifts," or "emergency pliers and toenail cleaner." I have a better use for the nut pick: to open old-style warded house locks.

4. Safety pin, #2 (1 1/2 inches long), closed. This is used for tight keyways and small pin-tumbler locks, such as dainty padlocks. It should be shaped to the same form as item 1 but downscaled, of course.

5. Small paper clip. Used by day as a mild-mannered paper collector, the paper clip moonlights as a lock picker. It is still used throughout the world for opening wooden-desk and antique-furniture locks. The small paper clip is used in conjunction with its daddy, the next item on this list.

6. Large paper clip L pick. Shown ready to work with its business end exposed, this lock pick is discussed later in the book and will be referred to as the L pick. It is also used on one- and two-lever suitcases, jewelry boxes, and some padlocks.

7. Large paper clip shown at his day job.

8. Bobby pin. This modest "girl," cleverly disguised as an ordinary hair stylist, is in fact the ultimate handcuff lock pick: locksmiths have been unable to come up with a better pick key for police handcuffs.

9. Wire coat hanger T pick. This is made from .073-inch-diameter (or less) hardened wire. Dry cleaners hand out these cheap, thin hangers with the cardboard tubes across the middle, which is what we want (and all this time you thought the damn things were useless). A vise is carefully used to make the tight bend at the end of the pick. This one is a bit tough to make within the dimension of just under .250-inch (1/4-inch) wide at the top of the T. But this "hammerhead shark" can open any warded padlock out there.

10. Tube pick, made from 1/4-inch-OD standard copper tubing. This tool is for opening barrel key locks used in old (and newly refurbished) antique desks, dressers, and liquor cabinets. This old lock has been revived and is in wide use again.

TOOL MAKING

The Pick

To make a safety-pin hook pick, first you need a large #3 safety pin (2 inches long). In a pinch you can use a #2 (1 1/2 inches long), but for guys with big, farmboy hands like mine, the larger #3 pin is easier to work. However, this safety pin is seldom used around the average home because its exaggerated size draws attention to such obvious boo-boos, such as ripped-out britches.

Carefully open the safety pin and spread it out to the angle shown in Figure 1, which shows the #3 size. Then curve its tip with a pair of pliers as shown. Next, draw the tip across a file (or carefully across a concrete sidewalk) to flatten it and round off any sharp edges to reduce the risk of impaling yourself. Compare the size with that of the one in the drawing (all tools shown in Figure 1 are exact size inside line).

This homemade lock pick may occasionally bend on you, but just use the keyhole of the lock you are picking to re-form the pick to the shape above. If you are using it where the temperature is below 32° Fahrenheit (0° Celsius), use caution when bending it: it may break off in the lock. Warm it up in your hand for a few minutes at first or use a cigarette lighter.

WARNING: Always wear safety glasses when making tools!

The Wrench

Pin- and wafer-cylinder locks need a tension wrench to apply a slight turning force on the cylinder while the lock is being picked. This replaces the function of the turning key once the tumblers are all aligned. Acquire a small flat-blade screwdriver (the kind electrical, plumbing, and other supply stores give away or sell cheap). See Figure 1, item 2 for exact size. You can also use a Stanley model #64-840 or the Stanley generic 2-inch (50mm)-long blade. If you can't find one of these, check your local

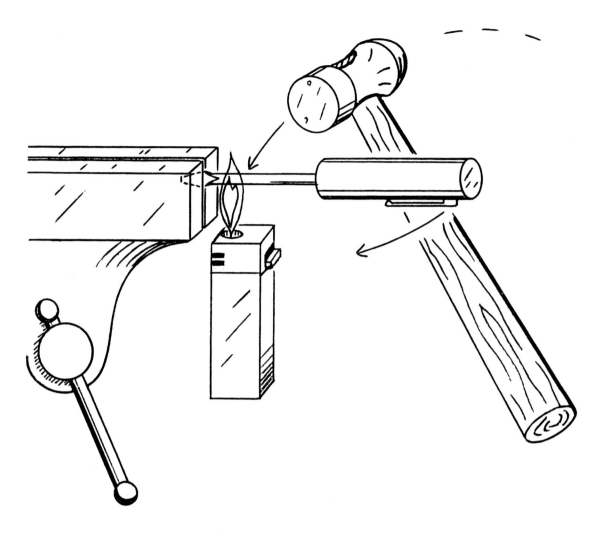

FIGURE 2
Making a tension wrench.

hardware stores. The blade tip must fit cleanly into the bottom of a pin-tumbler lock's keyway.

In Figure 2, the small, pocket, flat-blade screwdriver is placed horizontally (from the side) into a vise to make a tension wrench. Heat the blade with a cigarette lighter, being careful not to roast a finger or thumb. Place the tip of the *blue part* of the flame at the point where the blade is going to be bent, as shown. This is the hottest part of a flame and softens the hardened steel of the screwdriver shaft to make bending easier. (Without its being heated, the steel blade could

break.) After 30 seconds of heat, quickly tap the place on the screwdriver shaft, marked with an arrow in Figure 2 (while lightly pushing the screwdriver handle with your hand), using a hammer to make short, staccato taps. Tap until the shaft approaches the angle of 90 degrees (right-angle bend)[1] and let cool. *Remember to hold the screwdriver's handle while tapping so that it will not fly out of the vise.*

Remove the blade from the vise and check. If it is not OK, repeat the process outlined above. If it is all right, replace the handle in the vise,

---

[1] Even though the illustrations do not show it, you can make your tension-wrench angle less sharp—-anywhere from 45 to 70 degrees to better facilitate opening knob-set locks not covered in this book. But for beginners, 90 degrees works best. I personally like 55 degrees (about a third from a 90-degree bend), but this angle demands a twisting action and more skill with the wrench hand than with just pulling down on the cylinder. However, it does allow you to get into deep-set cylinders, such as those on vending machines, and high security padlocks).

lightly clamped, and heat the bend again for another 30 seconds; then *extinguish the lighter* to prevent a fire. Immediately afterward, squirt a small stream of 3-in-1 household oil over the heated area to temper it. It will smoke a bit, but that's all right. Let it cool and wipe the blade clean with rubbing alcohol and a paper towel. The metal will be black where you bent and re-tempered it, but this tension wrench is now ready to be used on nearly all cylinder locks that you will be picking. It is also hard enough to be used as a mini-pry bar in emergencies (use caution during this application because handles often break, causing injury.)

L and T Picks

The L pick is used to open lever locks, such as those in old handcuffs. The short (horizontal) leg of the L pick must be made to the proper length to fit into the keyway of the lever lock (see Figure 1, item 6.) You can make this simple pick by bending the tip of a large safety pin with a pair of pliers to a right angle. It is best to heat it first with a cigarette lighter and then pound it flat with a hammer on a vise, making it flare to twice its wire width. Trim off excess length of the short leg with wire cutters made for steel, or you can use a file or, best yet, a small electric grinder. If you have none of these trimming tools, use this cheap, yet effective method: carefully drag the tip across a concrete sidewalk (being careful not to drag your knuckles across the sidewalk as well; I know from experience that this smarts). Also, be sure to remove sharp edges. Compare the resulting size with that of item 6 in Figure 1.

If you're in a hurry, you can form a paper clip to suit. Insert the end of the extended paper clip into a crack, crevice, or small hole and bend the clip into the L-shape needed (for single-lever locks, you do not need to flatten the end of the pick.) You then can actuate the lever tumblers of a small padlock, suitcase lock, or even handcuffs.

The T pick is used to open warded padlocks, such as the Master laminated warded padlock series. There are two basic pick sizes used to open all these types of locks, and this will be discussed in detail later. But in Figure 1, item 9, the tool ends are of two sizes: 7/32 inch (as shown) and 9/32 (not shown). Here also, if you are hard-pressed for quality tool time, use the above method for the quickie paper clip L pick. The warded lock can be opened with the L tool, but this requires more skill and a bit more time.

Chapter 2
LOCK IDENTIFICATION

The first step to picking a lock is to know the type of lock to be opened. Obviously not all locks are alike. Over the centuries, in an effort to achieve higher security, many locks have come and gone. So, in a sense, locks have evolved with us humans—some functioning to fill needs and thereby enduring, with others failing to provide the required security and falling out of favor. If anything is to survive, it must adapt to its environment. So the locks we'll be covering have adapted quite well to their various niches.

Each lock, no matter how simple, serves a purpose. For example, it would not be practical to install a five-pin-tumbler cylinder lock on a jewelry box: the mechanism would be too bulky and cumbersome, outweighing the box, and such variety in keying is not needed. Conversely, you would not want a jewelry box lock on your front door because the greater the use, the more variation in keys needed (not to mention the need for greater durability). This also ensures that your neighbor does not have a key to your door. The differences in needs account for the wide variety of locks in use today; this chapter covers many of these locks.

Now, let's look at the 11 basic keyways of the 15 lock types covered in this book. In Figure 3 we see that not all locks are created equal. Let's review them.

1. Handcuff lock (one-lever, barrel ward). The earliest version of this type of shackle lock that I found was invented in the 1800s and looked like a steel U bolt mounted to a very low profile lock casing made of brass. One end of the U swiveled, and the locking end was secured by threads using a tube key with a cross-section shaped like a C. Apparently prisoners figured out the principle of the screw, and the lock went extinct. Shackles became more sophisticated in the early 1900s and were locked with a right-angled wafer-type cylinder lock (Figure 3, item 4) based on the invention of Linus Yale Jr.'s pin-tumbler lock (Figure 3, item 5). But the cylinder had a tendency to become corroded and to jam from sweat, dirt, and skin debris, making this type of shackle impractical. Finally a simple, single-lever, paw-like mechanism (the keyway depicted as item 1) won out. Here a drop in security was traded for dependability. In the 1970s, Smith and Wesson developed the modern and dependable stainless-steel police handcuff locking mechanism (covered later) employing three moving parts that must be actuated in sequence before the cuffs can be opened.

2. Warded house lock (one-lever, dead-bolt, flat ward). Contrary to popular belief, this lock can be a bitch to pick. Many "locksmiths" know how to pop a pin- or wafer-cylinder lock and can even open a warded house lock with a trusty "skeleton key." But lock them up behind an old-fashioned warded house lock with a coat hanger and they'd be in there for days. Generally these locks, though deceptively simple in design, require some knowledge and a little bit of skill to open. They will be covered later as well.

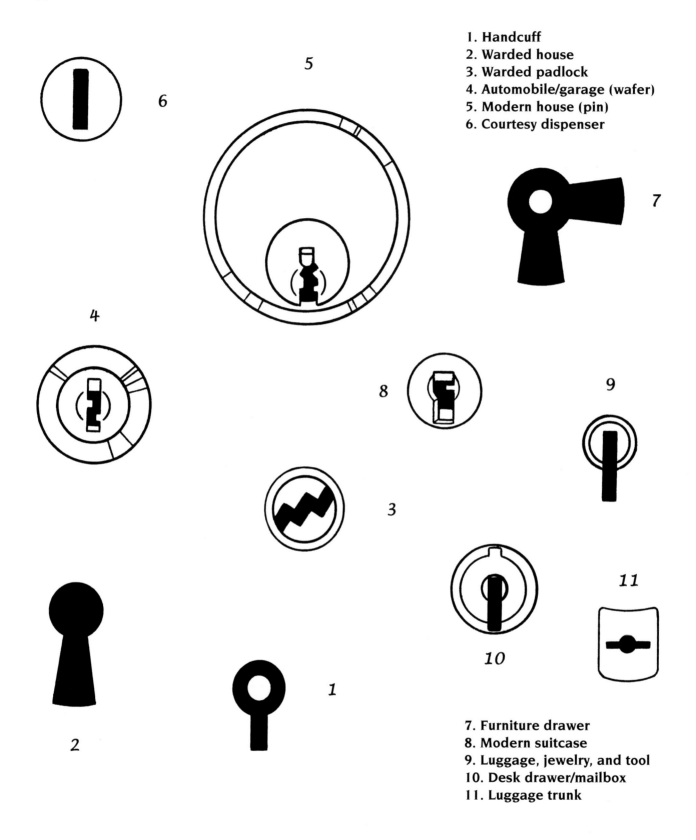

1. Handcuff
2. Warded house
3. Warded padlock
4. Automobile/garage (wafer)
5. Modern house (pin)
6. Courtesy dispenser

7. Furniture drawer
8. Modern suitcase
9. Luggage, jewelry, and tool
10. Desk drawer/mailbox
11. Luggage trunk

FIGURE 3
Lock keyway identification.

3. Warded padlock (two-spring-lever, flat ward). In the past 40 years, I've seen many warded padlocks slip into extinction—some brand names long lost from memory. Others like Hurd, Samson, and Sterling are only found in antique stores. Some companies survived but no longer make this type of lock, such as Corbin, Slaymaker, and Yale. However, the Master Lock Company still cranks out a very good line of these locks. Later, we'll see what makes them pop.

4. Automobile/garage lock (five-wafer cylinder). This lock is used everywhere, even on time clocks and small fire safes. Working on the principle of the pin tumbler lock (item 5), this mechanism uses a series of flat wafers, each holding a side-mounted spring that must be aligned by a key to clear their cylinder shear line.

5. Modern house lock (five-pin cylinder). The staple in modern security, this lock has evolved into a myriad of other higher security locks. Here, we only concern ourselves with the common pin tumbler house lock.

6. Courtesy dispenser cabinet lock (two-lever, two-bit key). This is used in public restroom paper towel and toilet paper dispensers. Don't laugh; this lock is a good one to know.

7. Furniture drawer lock (one-bolt, barrel ward). A recent revival in antique furniture restoration has led to the wide use of this type of lock. Also, many unrestored dressers and cabinet doors still use it.

8. Modern suitcase lock (two-row, two-wafer cylinder). This lock was developed because of the inadequacies of the next group of locks.

9. Luggage, jewelry, and tool box (one- and two-lever). The lever lock has been around for a few centuries, and many examples of these have also gone extinct, such as Acme, Buck, Miloco, and Reese padlocks. Such brands as Crest and a few surviving Master padlocks are still used today because of their adaptability. They can be fitted in small, confined places; they offer modest security and are cheap to make.

10. Desk drawer and mailbox (two-lever, dead bolt). As luck would have it, this very simple lock is rated highest for flat tumbler security within the parameters of this book. You'll find out why as I show you how to pick this lock.

11. Luggage trunk lock (one-spring-lever, dead latch). Though this old lock has been around a while, few people know how easy it is to pick.

Chapter 3
PIN-TUMBLER LOCKS

Modern pin-tumbler locks have been in use for more than 150 years and are considered to provide upper-medium security. Based on the 4,500-year-old Egyptian wooden-peg locks, the modern version was invented by Linus Yale Sr. in the 1820s. His son, Linus Yale Jr., perfected the lock by making it cylindrical. Now they are used worldwide for houses, Ford automobiles, padlocks, alarm boxes, filing cabinets, parking meters, machinery switches, and lockboxes.

PRINCIPLE OF OPERATION

Figure 4 shows a front and side view of a pin-tumbler lock with and without a key inserted. The pin-tumbler lock works on a simple principle: a cylinder (7) with a key slot machined down its length, is housed within a shell (5). This cylinder also has holes to accommodate a series of bottom (3) and top pins (2), which are held down by tumbler springs (1) in the upper section of the shell (5). When the proper key (8) is inserted into the cylinder, it aligns all the bottom pins (3) so that their top surfaces are level with the cylinder-shell shear line (6). This allows the key to turn freely, turning the cam (4) with it and thus unlocking the lock.

PICKING THE PIN-TUMBLER LOCK

In picking this lock, the pick and tension wrench simply replace the function of the key. The pick sets the tumblers one by one while the tension wrench supplies a slight angular force on the cylinder to hold the picked pins in place. Once all the pins are set, the wrench acts as a key, turning the cylinder to move the cam at the back of the lock.

Examine the X-ray view of the pin-tumbler lock being picked in Figure 5. With a large, bent safety pin as shown, locate the very first pin; you can see it by looking down the keyway. Get beneath it with this "pick" and you should be able to raise it up. It is spring-loaded and will snap back down when you release it. Now raise it again and try to gently insert the pick farther into the lock to engage the next pin. You'll feel it because it too is spring-loaded.

Now release both pins and slip the pick all the way back into the lock as shown in Figure 5. Place the small bent screwdriver—the tension wrench—into the bottom of the keyway as shown, being careful not to interfere with your pick. Do not apply any force to the tension wrench. Slowly pull the pick out until you feel the very last pin's spring tension against your pick.

Now release that pin and apply a slight turning pressure with the tension wrench on the cylinder to cause the pins to bind a bit. Raise the back tumbler until it clicks into place. *Do not raise it any farther after it clicks.*

Remember to go very easy with the wrench. Use a force similar to that used for turning a page. If the pins are not staying in place as you raise them, increase the wrench pressure ever so slightly until the pins begin to stay in place. Maintain this pressure throughout the picking process.

Now gently pull the pick out until you engage the next to last tumbler and repeat the process. Then do the same with the last three tumblers, working your way out of the lock until the

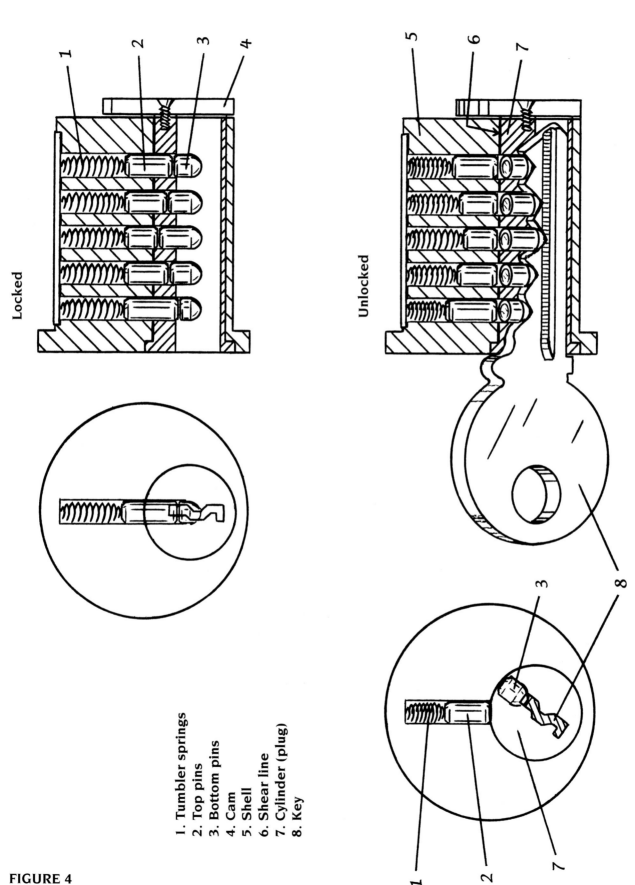

Locked

Unlocked

1. Tumbler springs
2. Top pins
3. Bottom pins
4. Cam
5. Shell
6. Shear line
7. Cylinder (plug)
8. Key

FIGURE 4
Pin-tumbler lock.

Click!

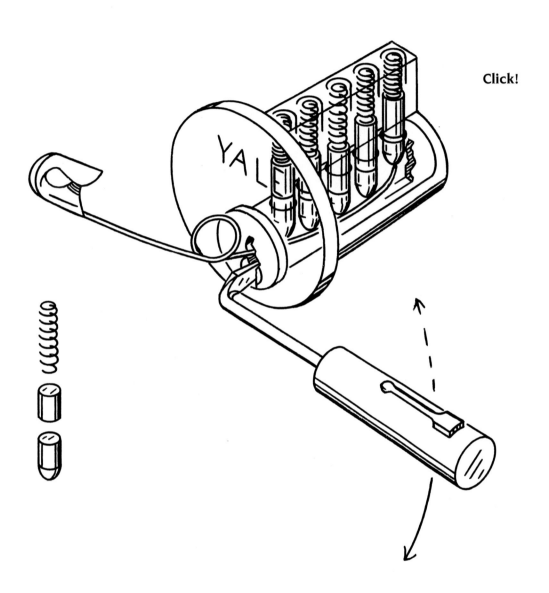

FIGURE 5
Picking a pin-tumbler lock.

cylinder releases. When this happens, the cylinder will snap free, unlocking the lock.

HELPFUL TIPS

I revolutionized lock picking by teaching the "back tumbler first" technique. This is based on simple physics: the torque that is ever so gently applied to the front of the cylinder with the tension wrench is going to bind the last tumbler the most simply because the tumbler is farthest from the angle of applied torque. Because of this slight deviation in the incidence of the cylinder caused by the tension-wrench hand, the last pin is the most likely to bind, placing it at a "twisted" disadvantage when the cylinder is turned. So you can feel the cylinder give way with every move of the pick as you work each tumbler into place on your way out of the lock. This technique also prevents interference with tumblers that have already been set.

Now, if you raise a tumbler too far, you'll also feel it in the tension-wrench hand (mostly in the fingers), and you'll have to release the tension-wrench pressure and start over again. This is because like the tumbler that is too low, the extended tumbler also will not allow the cylinder to turn.

The direction to turn the tension wrench to unlock the cylinder depends on the lock and how it is mounted, but generally most pin-tumbler locks unlock clockwise to the right. If that doesn't open it, then you have to go the opposite direction with the wrench. As you gain experience, you will sense which direction to turn the wrench. But the best general clue is that most pin-tumbler locks will not allow the pins to bind if they are being picked in the wrong direction. For pin-tumbler dead-bolt locks (mounted directly in the door), the top of the keyway turns toward the door's hinges. In knob-set locks, they can go in either direction.

Sometimes you may have to pick the pins randomly because a middle or back pin may break high up into the shell. This will depend on the way the lock is keyed. If there is a long top pin, there will be little room to manipulate the pins behind it because of its long profile, so the safety-pin pick is less likely to jam than professional picks. Still, it does happen. This is where your tension wrench plays an important part.

The classic Yale five-pin tumbler dead-bolt lock with improvised lock picks. Remember to angle the safety-pin pick to accommodate the slant of the keyway.

Many professionals, including experienced locksmiths, believe that the "magic touch" to picking a lock is in the way the fingers hold the pick. Wrong. The magic hand is the one holding the tension wrench. A thumb-and-forefinger hold is sufficient. If you have the touch with the wrench, then you can open just about any lock you encounter. This entails knowing how much (if any) relief to give the wrench as each tumbler is picked, as well as when to give relief. If a tumbler is pushed up too far, a proper wrench hand with a subtle twist can release it without losing the setting of the other tumblers, thus saving time in opening the lock. But don't be discouraged at first—lock picking takes lots of practice.

I taught myself how to pick locks at age 15 and collected old, discarded locks. I made up a 2-by-3-foot wooden box and mounted them on it. After a while, it held about 70 different locks of various types: antique padlocks, beaten knob-set locks, rusty furniture locks, forsaken combination padlocks abandoned by schools, whored-out pin-tumbler cylinders of unknown origins—anything I

Though its case looks like a simple lever lock, the #77 Master padlock holds a small four-pin tumbler cylinder.

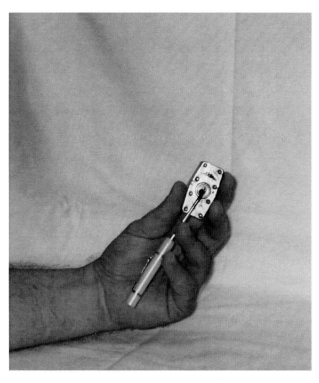

The underhand grip allows you to hold a pin-tumbler padlock with the tension wrench hand.

could get my hands on that locked was on that box. Locks even hung from the sides. It looked like some coffin from "lock hell"—where bad locks go. But each night, I'd try to pick as many of those locks as possible before going to bed. In a few years, I could open any one of them in moments using the simple tools I showed you at the beginning of this book.

If you can master the average pin-tumbler lock, such as the one on your front door (make sure you don't lock yourself out) with your homemade picks, then you will have no trouble with the rest of the locks in this book.

PIN-TUMBLER PADLOCKS

Pin-tumbler padlocks usually have only four pins and the cylinders are smaller than house locks, but they are picked the same way as pin door locks with the #2 safety-pin pick. However, they are not firmly mounted, so that picking them is not so easily accomplished. Padlocks have to be held with the hand that normally holds the tension wrench. I've been told by some locksmiths that it is impossible to pick a pin-tumbler padlock because, unless you are an octopus, there is no way to get a grip on the cylinder. This is not true. In fact, one old-time locksmith got very pissed off when I proved my argument right in front of him using my technique. Things were never quite the same between us again.

Another problem with pin-tumbler padlocks is that they are often used outside where the brass tumblers and cylinder can be corroded by moisture, causing the cylinders to be very tight. This reduces the picker's ability to sense the breaking tumblers while picking, and actually makes picking the pin-tumbler padlock even more difficult than picking a higher security-rated door-mounted house lock.

So oddly, in certain ways, pin-tumbler padlocks are more pick-resistant than pin tumbler house locks. But unfortunately for owners, such disadvantages as corroded cylinders often leads to broken-off keys in the padlock, which means having to cut the lock's shackle. Still, a dangling padlock can prevent the common picklock from trying his luck on a storage unit or garage.

IN THE PALM OF YOUR HAND

To pick a weathered pin-tumbler padlock (if you are right-handed) hold the body of the lock in your left hand (underhand grip, palm up) with the keyhole facing up. With your right hand, insert the tension wrench, and with the last two fingers of your left hand (ring and little finger), hold down the handle of the wrench while you pick the tumblers with your right hand. If you have large hands, you can use the overhand grip (palm down) and use your index finger to push the wrench. This is good if your hand gets fatigued with the underhand grip. Remember, you may have to maintain a stiffer tension wrench because of corrosion. More experience and skill are needed to open outside pin padlocks.

You may squirt a spritz of Liquid Wrench into the tumblers and the cylinder walls and give the padlock a few good raps with a large screwdriver handle or other firm object to loosen the works. This makes picking the pin-tumbler padlock much easier, but you then lose the element of stealth and leave evidence, since this substance is a light lubricant and will stain the lock for years to come. If you own brass pin-tumbler padlocks that are out in the elements, squirt this substance into them once every 3 years to keep them in good shape (stainless-steel pin-tumbler padlocks do not require this because they do not corrode). But it may be better to risk having the lock picked rather than breaking off a key when you need to get in. Also this reduces overall wear on the brass parts of the lock. Be certain that the

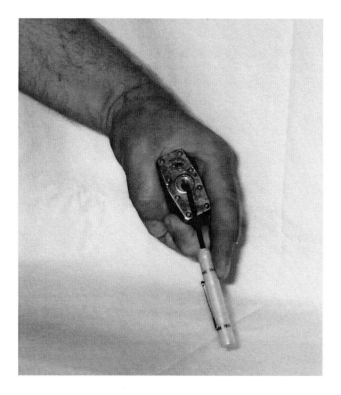

The overhand grip gives a little less control but is good for relieving hand and finger fatigue while picking the pin-tumbler padlock.

padlock's keyway hangs down so that water and moisture can drain out.

If you need a good padlock to weather the years, buy an ABUS discus padlock. This German-made, stainless-steel, spool-pinned tumbler lock is considered high security. (I reviewed it in *Modern High-Security Locks*, available from the Web site listed in the back of this book.) The lock has a shouldered or shrouded shackle to prevent bolt-cutter-happy thieves from separating it from its hasp—and you from your belongings.

Chapter 4
WAFER-TUMBLER LOCKS

Wafer-tumbler locks are of medium security and have been in existence for more than 80 years. Also universally used, these locks can be found on desk drawers, cabinets, freezers, older automobile ignition switches, garage doors, and small fire safes.

PRINCIPLE OF OPERATION

Figure 6 shows an exploded view of a wafer-tumbler lock. Note that unlike the round pins of a pin-tumbler lock, these tumblers are flat with a tang on the side that contacts a spring. As the key enters the cylinder, it goes *through* the wafers, taking up less space than a pin-tumbler arrangement. This means the lock has about half the security of a pin-tumbler lock (there are fewer variations of wafers—about five instead of 10 different tumbler cuts on the standard pin-tumbler lock)— but the advantage is that it can be used in tighter places than a pin-tumbler lock. Wafers are also easier to manufacture than pins, so this brings the price of the lock down as well: wafers are stamped out with a punch press, while pins have to be machined or "turned down" on lathes.

In Figure 6, a series of flat wafers (3), held up within the cylinder (2) by tumbler springs (4), protrude into the complementary recess (flat groove with dashed line going through it) inside the shell (5). When the key (1) enters the keyway of the cylinder (2), through the wafers (3), it aligns the wafers against the force of their springs (4). This allows the ends of the wafers to clear the shear line between the cylinder and shell, freeing the cylinder to turn.

PICKING A WAFER-TUMBLER LOCK

Basically wafer-tumbler locks are picked the same way as pin-tumbler locks. Locate the last tumbler (in this case, wafer) in the plug with your safety-pin lock pick and apply your tension wrench at the bottom of the keyway. Figure 7 shows a wafer-tumbler cylinder as it is picked.

Next, these tumblers are thinner than pin tumblers, so they are closer together. Sometimes these locks are mounted upside down, so your tools have to be inverted as shown in Figure 7. Depress the last tumbler until it clicks into place and work your way out of the cylinder until it pops.

Again, if you move a tumbler too far past its breaking point (click), the cylinder will not turn to unlock the lock. This principle holds true for all cylinder locks, for that matter. But here, referring back to the exploded view in Figure 6, the wafer (3) goes *through* the plug (2) and extends out the bottom, where it will engage a recessed groove along the inner length of the lock's shell (5). This in effect locks the cylinder (plug) up from the bottom instead of the top, so push the wafer down with your pick only until it clicks and no farther.

The direction the cylinder turns depends on the application and manufacturer, but usually the tumblers will not stick if you are going the wrong direction with the tension wrench. NOTE: GM automobile wafer locks use a "side bar" to isolate the tumblers from shear line. These require special tools and picking techniques (see *Modern High-Security Locks*, Chapter 5, on side-bar locks).

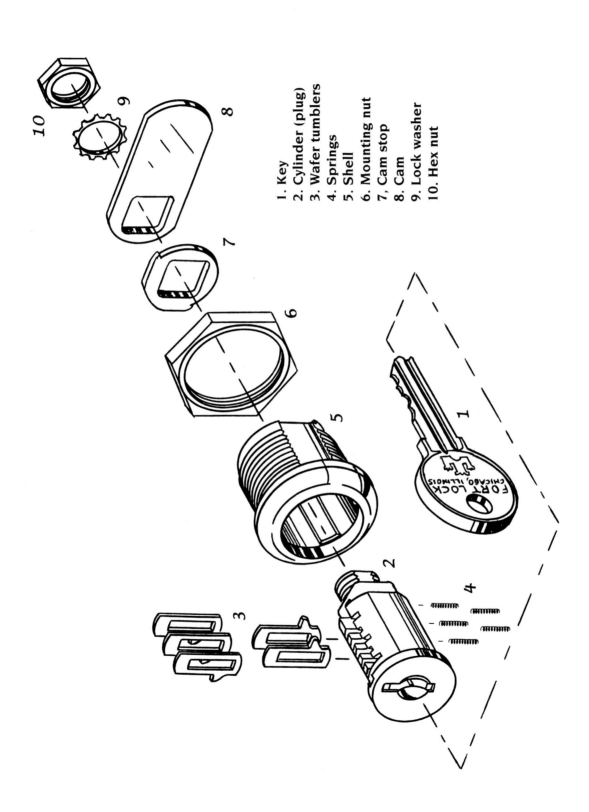

1. Key
2. Cylinder (plug)
3. Wafer tumblers
4. Springs
5. Shell
6. Mounting nut
7. Cam stop
8. Cam
9. Lock washer
10. Hex nut

Courtesy of Fort Lock

FIGURE 6
Wafer-tumbler lock.

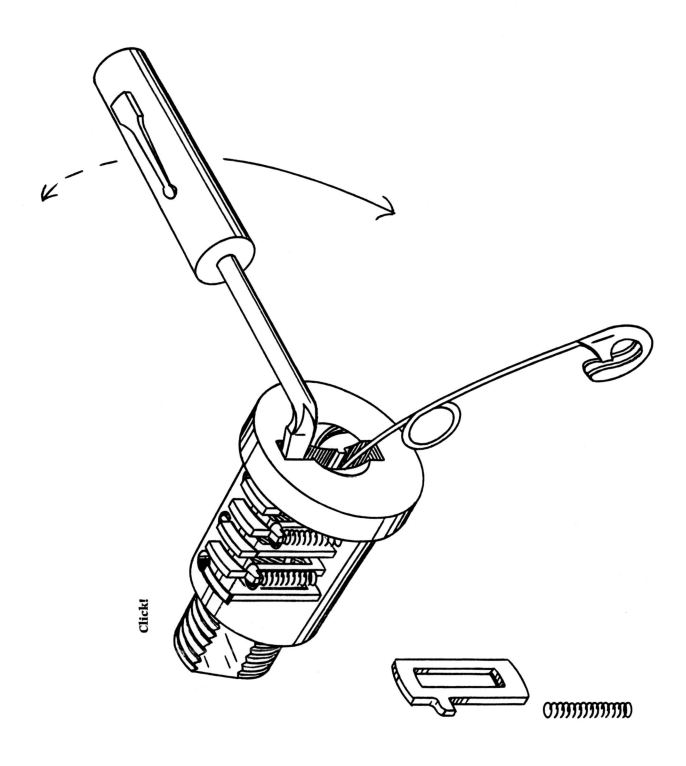

Click!

FIGURE 7
Picking a wafer-tumbler lock.

The Fort Lock's burglar alarm switch lock is also used on tractors and industrial machinery. The cylinder is identical to that of the lock in Figure 6.

The Royal suitcase with the widely used double-row wafer, two-tumbler cylinder lock (see Figure 8).

MODERN SUITCASE LOCKS

Luggage security is always a matter of personal privacy while on the move or away from home, and most older suitcases require little time to pick. However, the traveler seldom loses sight of his luggage, except while it is being routed by baggage handlers at train stations or devoured by the handling systems in airports. And most pick thieves have run the gauntlet when it comes to the various lever locks on luggage, so Samsonite (subsequently Royal and other manufacturers) started putting the double-row, two-wafer-tumbler lock on their suitcases.

In the 1960s Samsonite ran TV commercials that showed another brand of locked suitcase being thrown into a cage with a gorilla. The bored gorilla would bang it open in moments, strewing clothes everywhere. Then a Samsonite suitcase (loaded with bananas to keep him interested) was thrown in, and the gorilla would give it a good working over. The suitcase stayed locked

and closed, frustrating the poor fellow. This demonstrated that single-lever locks could be sprung open with enough force in the right place. But by using dual wafers that are spring-loaded in opposite directions, no matter the direction of force, one of the wafers will always be in the latched position. Thus became the *double-row* wafer suitcase lock.

In Figure 8, note that the two wafers (1) share one tumbler spring (2), thus conserving space. The back tumbler must move down, and the front tumbler must move up before the cylinder (3) can turn, arcing the peg cam (4) that protrudes out its back. This peg runs through a slot on both hook latches (5) and causes them to compress to center and lower. The two hook latches also share a common latch spring (6), a leaf spring that joins the latches across their bottom edges.

In Figure 8 we see that more than one tool is needed to open these locks. Pick this one as you would a standard wafer-tumbler cylinder; however, after picking the back wafer, you must remove the pick and run it into the keyway right

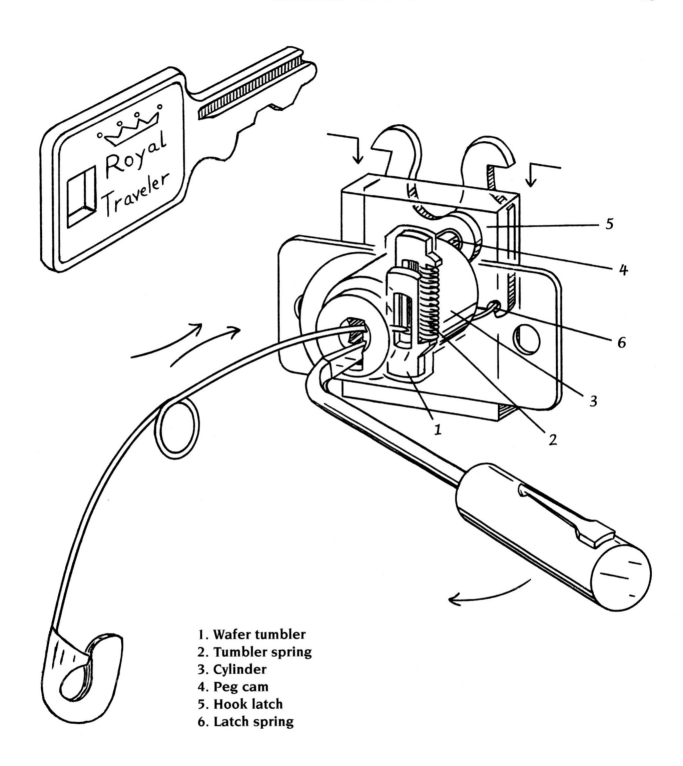

1. Wafer tumbler
2. Tumbler spring
3. Cylinder
4. Peg cam
5. Hook latch
6. Latch spring

FIGURE 8
Modern suitcase lock (double-row wafer, two-tumbler cylinder).

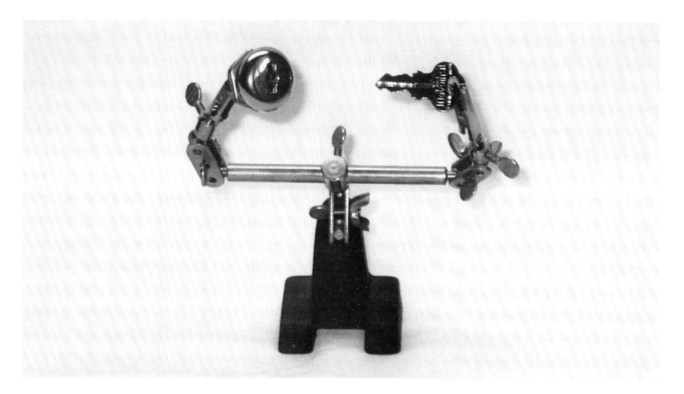

Chicago Lock's double-row wafer, six-tumbler cylinder suitcase lock uses three breaking wafers on the top and three on the bottom of the cylinder. This lock is picked like the one in Figure 8, except the pick must be inserted a little deeper into the lock to reach the additional two sets of tumblers.

side up to engage the front wafer tumbler. This particular Royal lock will retract the hooks and set them down into the lock when the cylinder is turned and the key is removed 180 degrees later. The keyway is small, so you will have to set your tension wrench out, using the very tip of it to engage the cylinder.

Use caution and a steady wrench hand so that you do not strip metal off the face of the keywell by letting the wrench slip out. You should be able to pick the bottom *and* top wafers without having to remove the wrench, but you will have to remove and reverse your pick.

Samsonite and Royal use the same double-wafer cylinder mechanism. In fact the key blanks are directly interchangeable (both locks are made by the same manufacturer). However, newer Samsonite suitcases use two of these cylinders with a less complex cam-like latch on each side of the suitcase that must snap up when the cylinder has been turned.

Some tool and equipment case manufacturers use the standard five-wafer (discussed above) or the six-tumbler double-wafer lock—with three wafers breaking on top and three breaking on bottom. These pick the same as the above lock, but you have to place the tension wrench in the center of the keyway and pick deeper into the lock (for more information, see *Secrets of Lock Picking*, Paladin Press). But here I cover only the common two-wafer suitcase lock.

Chapter 5
SINGLE-LEVER LOCKS

We are going to retrograde. So far we have examined the two major tumbler locks in use today, the pin- and wafer-tumbler *cylinder* locks. However, approximately 25 percent of the locks in use around the world today are *not* cylinder locks and are classified as *flat-tumbler* locks.

THE LEGACY OF FLAT-TUMBLER LOCKS

Flat-tumbler locks have secured man's treasures for more than 5 centuries. Yet many locksmiths don't know how to pick the majority of these old, simple locks. Furthermore, my guess is there's another 15 percent of new flat-tumbler locks in use today as high-security devices that even fewer people know how to open. These locks are gradually replacing standard pin- and wafer-tumbler cylinder locks in high-risk applications. We will cover just the simple locks here, not the newer high-security ones.

CLASSIFYING THE CLASSICS

Let's start with the simplest flat-tumbler locks and work our way up through the more complex lever and warded locks. But first the matter of classification. I have arranged these next groups of locks in logical sequence when possible. However, there is some confusion in the locksmith community about how lever locks and warded locks should be classified.

Wards are often used in lever locks to restrict rogue or otherwise wrong keys from engaging the lever tumblers or throw bolt. Warded locks sometimes have lever tumblers but not always: warded padlocks use lever-type springs to hold

the shackle closed and do not use a bolt other than the shackle, which technically is a bolt. But the proper key for the warded padlock does not directly engage the bolt, a distinction from warded house locks and other multiple-lever dead-bolt locks. Also, some lever locks, such as furniture and handcuff locks, use wards to restrict keying and as lock pick obstacles.

So to simplify things, I have classified the lever lock into five basic groups: simple *single-lever* (some small padlocks, suitcase and luggage zipper locks); *double-lever* (public courtesy cabinets and lever padlocks); *single-lever, barrel ward* (furniture doors and handcuffs); *single-lever, dead-bolt, flat ward* (old-style house locks and laminated padlocks); and the dastardly *double-lever, dead bolt* (wooden desks and steel lockers).

A Single Lever Secured the World

An upper-low security lock in use for about 250 years, single-lever locks are used on old cabinets, jewelry boxes, courtesy paper dispensers, older suitcases, luggage, zippers, and small padlocks. For me to be overly explicit with this group of locks would insult your intelligence, but I will review these simple mechanisms briefly.

Zipper Locks

Now, you may be wondering what possible use a zipper lock could serve. If you are a man reading this, the concept is a bit unsettling. If you are a woman reading this, you may think it a good idea. But for us guys, a zipper lock provokes the image of lost keys and a frantic race to the nearest pair of wire cutters. Just to be clear, we

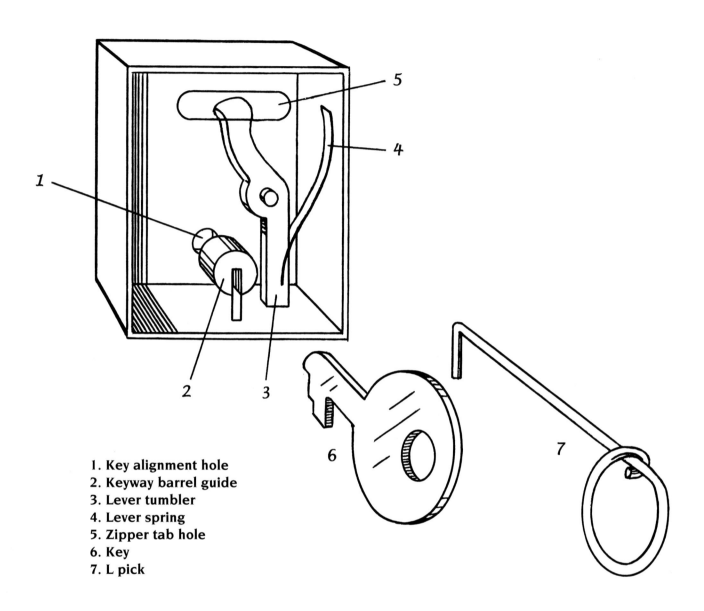

1. Key alignment hole
2. Keyway barrel guide
3. Lever tumbler
4. Lever spring
5. Zipper tab hole
6. Key
7. L pick

FIGURE 9
Luggage zipper, small padlock (single lever).

are *not* talking about *fly* zipper locks here, but *luggage* zipper locks.

Figure 9 shows a very basic zipper lock. Item 1 is the key alignment hole that stabilizes the end of the key like one end of an axle bearing block. All simple lever locks use such a hole. The keyway barrel guide (2) keeps the bit of the key aligned with the lever tumbler (3), which must be moved against the force of its spring (4). The zipper tab (handle) slips into the top opening (5) of the lock housing and is held in place by the lever (3). Note that the key (6) is needed to allow the zipper tab to be inserted into the lock. This prevents accidentally locking the key in the carrier. Luggage zipper locks are used on travel valet suit carriers and soft briefcases.

The lock depicted in Figure 9 is the basic mechanism also used in small and often older padlocks. These small lever padlocks are sometimes found on such large pieces of luggage as sea bags, trunks using hasps, and utility and old toolboxes. They open under the same principle: a simple lever with a hooked end holds down a spring-loaded shackle. They hardly ever use a restricting ward or keyway and are very easy to pick.

To pick this lock, simply insert an L pick (7) and twist it to the right and left until you feel the lever and then depress to release the shackle.

Luggage Trunk and Jewelry Box Locks

The next group of locks also use the basic lever, but the lever does not directly release the latch. In some applications you want to leave the latch in an unlocked position but still be able to close the lid of a box, for example.

Today people seldom use jewelry boxes that lock; anything of value is secured in something that is large and heavy, such as a safe. So unless he can take on Arnold Schwarzenegger, the thief is not likely to tuck the family jewels under a trench coat and walk out the front door. But a few companies still make these dinky lockboxes, and you may have to pick one open for a little girl who has lost her keys.

Another lockbox of sorts is the luggage trunk. Older luggage trunk locks, many of which are still in use around the world, also work on the same principle as the basic jewelry box lock. This mechanism functions with a spring-lever that allows a dead-latching plate to release a cam once that lever is shifted to the unlocked position.

The L pick is also used to open these types of locks. First make the right size L pick for the lock you are about to open. You must be able to slide it in without catching on the bottom of the keyway. Next, slowly rotate it about 45 degrees as you gently glide it in and out. This is how you search for the lever. For locks with simple levers, such as in Figure 9, you will feel the lever since it is spring-loaded and will give a little. If you come to an obstacle that will not give, do not turn further; this is a stationary ward or gate and will bend your tool, weakening it.

Referring to the trunk lock shown in Figure 10, remove the outer housing (7) to reveal the inner housing (6) of the lock. The spring-lever (1) is actually a flat-leaf spring, bent in a shape to also act as a dead bolt, resting on the latch stop (2), where it prevents the latch plate (4) from sliding down.[1] Since you are engaging the lever in its middle (action a), near the upper inside of the keyway (in the "hump"), there will be no springy feel to it. But once you have slid this spring-lever (1) to the right with your L pick (10, action b), you can push down on the button ward/latch (5), bringing down the latch plate (4, action c), which turns the right side of the cam (3, action d) down to release the hook bolt (8)— mounted on the lid of the enclosure. To relock the lock, slide the spring-lever (1) to the left, and the button ward/latch (5) cannot be lowered.

Also note that the key (9) is double-bit key even though this lock uses a single-lever-type mechanism. This is for customer convenience; the key can be inserted and used either upside down or right side up. The Ford Motor Company also uses a double-bit key (commonly referred to as the "drunkard's key") on all its five-pin-tumbler auto locks so that the key is not accidentally jammed into the lock upside down, causing broken keys or worse.

Some older luggage trunk locks have a single lever as well, and here there is little room to manipulate the lever. In most cases it is easier

---

[1] Technically, this lock could be classified as a spring-lever/dead-latch lock because the lever also is the latch. However, since the action involved with opening this lock is basically like that of a simple single-lever lock, I have termed it as such.

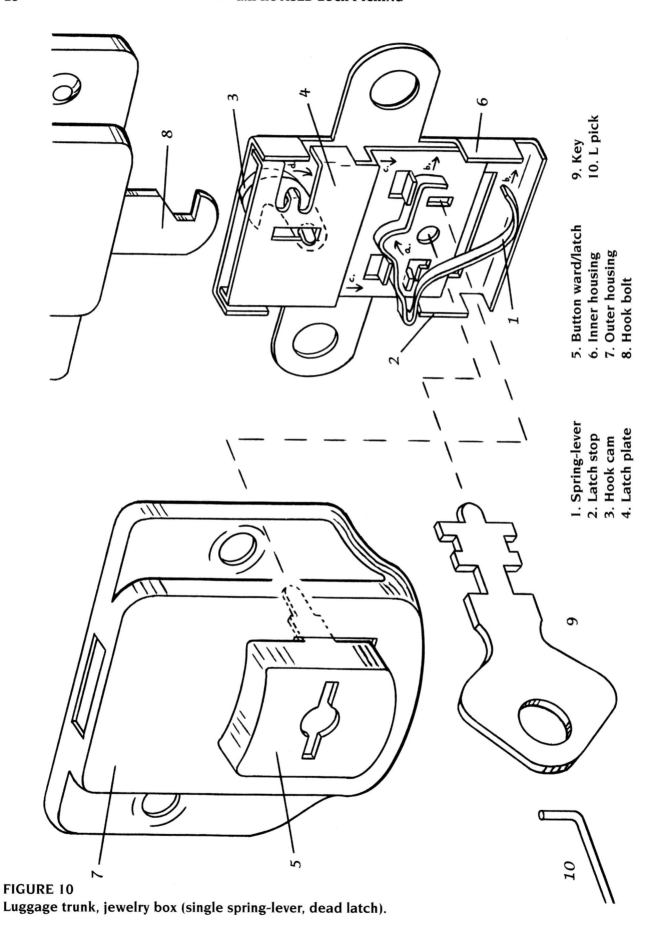

1. Spring-lever
2. Latch stop
3. Hook cam
4. Latch plate
5. Button ward/latch
6. Inner housing
7. Outer housing
8. Hook bolt
9. Key
10. L pick

FIGURE 10
Luggage trunk, jewelry box (single spring-lever, dead latch).

Chapter 6
DOUBLE-LEVER LOCKS

If one lever works well, maybe two levers will work *twice* as well. And they do. In fact two levers with a bolt can keep quite a few people locked out, as we'll see later on. But for now let's look at some basic two-lever mechanisms.

The #44 Master toolbox padlock, which uses a double-lever mechanism and ward slugs. This simple lock has frustrated many would-be picklock.

COURTESY CABINET LOCKS

These locks are classified as double-lever, double-bit key and are of low security. They can often be found on utility cabinets or such courtesy dispensers as for paper towels or toilet paper.

The principle is quite simple. Basically two spring-loaded levers have to be spread apart to be release from the catches. This lock, however, is not as hard to pick as *a two-lever single-bit lock*, since only one simple action is needed to open the former. Double-lever tumbler locks (next classification) have both levers side by side, making picking them a bit more difficult because each lever has a different distance to travel. In the double-bit lever lock the levers are opposite each other and simply have to be spread equally in opposite directions.

In Figure 11, the cabinet or box frame (1) holds the latch hook or catch (6). The movable cover (2) holds the rest of the mechanism. Once the key is inserted into the keyway barrel (3) and turned, spreading the levers (5), they become disengaged from the latch catches (6) and the lid or cover is free to open.

Here, we can use the T pick, and with one simple twist of the wrist have the lock opened. However, an L pick will work if you can move one lever over and cause it to stick while pulling on the container's lid to hold that lever in place. Then, you can move the other lever, which will pop the lid open. Sometimes a small screwdriver will work too, but you risk leaving telltale scratches in the keyway.

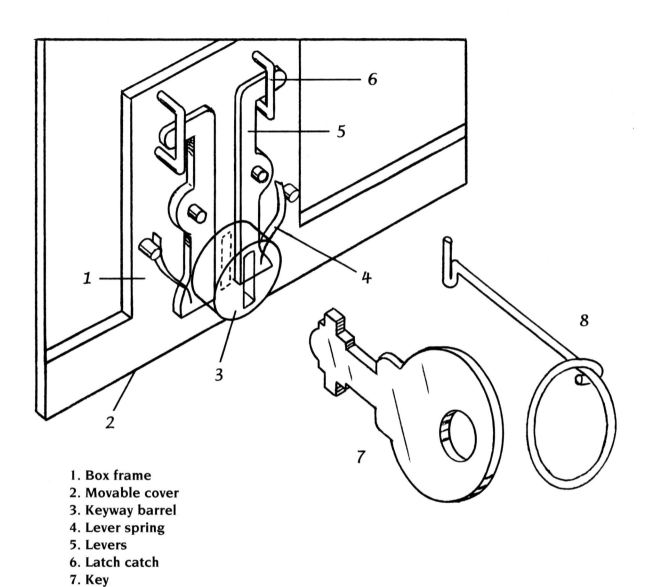

1. Box frame
2. Movable cover
3. Keyway barrel
4. Lever spring
5. Levers
6. Latch catch
7. Key
8. T pick

FIGURE 11
Courtesy cabinet lock (double lever, double-bit key).

1. Ward slug
2. Lever tumbler spring
3. Lever tumbler
4. Shackle
5. Shackle spring
6. Keyway
7. Key
8. Pick key
9. L pick

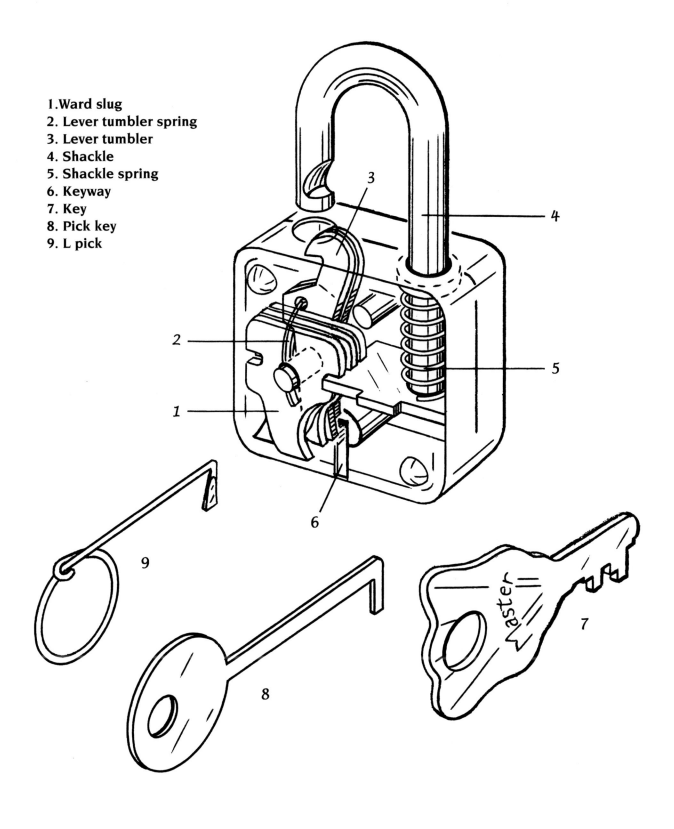

FIGURE 12
Toolbox padlock (double lever, single-bit key).

TOOLBOX PADLOCKS

The most common lever padlock today is the Master Lock Company's riveted-case, double-lever padlock, though the company is no longer making it. Because of their dependability, however, many are still in use today.

These locks came in three different sizes: #44, #55, and the #66 wrought-steel (stamped-out) case with riveted halves. You may run into one occasionally, especially in Europe, Southeast Asia, Canada, and rural parts of the United States.

In Figure 12, note the three ward slugs (1) in the front interior of the lock. These can be reversed and rearranged at the factory to give limited keying variations. The two levers (3) are at the back and may not be identical in width (this also is to give key variation). The lever tumbler spring (2) keeps tension on the lever, each lever having its own spring. From right to left we see the key for this lock (7), the locksmith's pick key (8), and a homemade L pick (9). Note how the key's bits align with the lock's wards and lever tumblers.

Referring to Figure 12, start by inserting your L pick (9) into the keyway (6) and feel for the spring-loaded lever tumblers (3). If you are careful, you can set one lever while gently pulling down on the padlock shackle, causing it to stick in place. Then locate and activate the other lever. Once you set the second lever tumbler, the shackle (4) pops open. Usually, the lock pops open ceremoniously with a snap once you engage both levers simultaneously. In this lock, the levers are not always in the back of the lock case and not always side by side.

Note that Master still makes this style of wrought-steel padlock casing, the Model #77, but it houses a small four-pin tumbler cylinder instead of the two-lever mechanism in Figure 12 and features a lion's head stamped on its front.

Chapter 7
BARREL-WARD LOCKS

The next group consists of locks that are slightly more complex and sometimes use two levers. This group covers antique dresser locks and handcuffs. These locks have an obstacle—namely a post at a very inconvenient place—in the middle of the keyway.

FURNITURE DOOR LOCKS

Figure 13 is a depiction of a typical antique furniture drawer lock still in use today. The lock's bolt also acts as the lever, and it is spring-loaded. This lock also has a flat ward, though not all such locks do.

Ilco/Unican is the only company that now makes barrel key blanks for antique furniture, and it carries 14 different styles of blanks. Sometimes it pays to visit antique shops and buy old barrel keys. I file mine down like that in Figure 13 (6) with a file or, more conveniently,

Antique dresser using the single-bolt, barrel-ward lock. Note the barrel wards in the center of each keyway. This dresser is more than 90 years old, and the locks still work smooth as silk.

Single-bolt, barrel-ward lock insert. These locks slip down into a mortised slot in each dresser drawer in the previous photo. Note bolt and bolt spring extending down past the lock's housing.

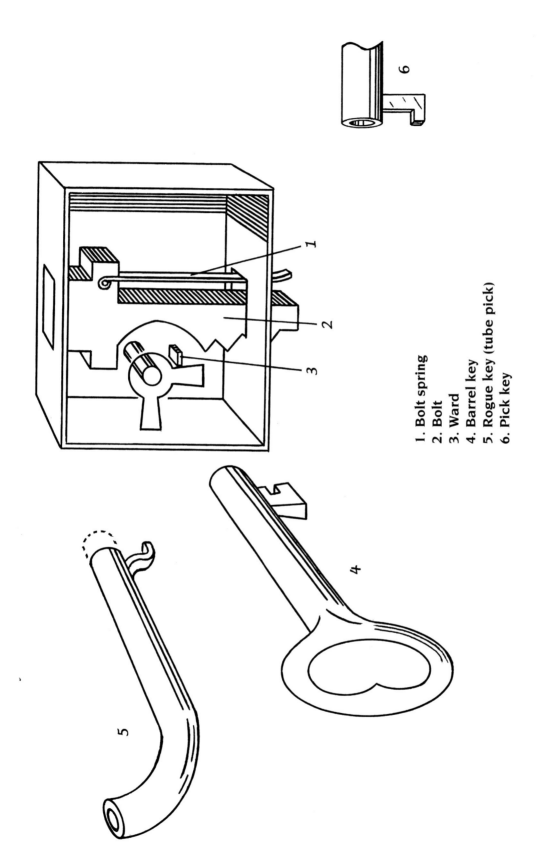

1. Bolt spring
2. Bolt
3. Ward
4. Barrel key
5. Rogue key (tube pick)
6. Pick key

FIGURE 13
Furniture drawer lock (single bolt, barrel ward).

with a small bench grinder cut-off wheel (see the author's other books in the bibliography for more details on making this and other tools). The key metal is potted, which is soft, so go easy with the powered cut-off wheel.

There is such a large variety of barrel key locks still found on older (as well as newer) furniture that to carry so many blanks would be impractical. So when Granny loses her key to her old antique dresser, we can temporarily make her a rogue key to at least get her in and even relock it for her until she can get a new key. Just remember that copper is soft, and the bit might break off in the lock if used too often.

The principle of operation is quite simple. The key (4) is probably the most complex part of the whole works. To lock this lock, the key is inserted and turned to the left (counterclockwise). The key's bit catches the curved surface of the bolt (2) and compresses the bolt spring (1). In so doing, the bolt is pushed to the right, allowing its toothed surface on the lower left to clear the lock case and latch the bolt in the locked position with the bolt up. The key can then be removed from the keyway and exit left of the barrel ward.

To unlock the lock the key (4), pick key (6), or adequate rogue key (5) is inserted and turned to the right (clockwise), pushing the bolt over and down to be latched in the retracted position. You can also use a nut pick on some of these locks and pick them as you would a large lever lock.

Figure 13 shows a simple rogue barrel key used to open old dresser locks. Use a piece of 1/4-inch copper tube and carefully cut with a hacksaw blade as indicated in the drawing. Wrap the bottom half of the blade with duct or masking tape and use that end as a handle. You'll have to make the tang (bit) the length to fit the lock you are trying to open as there are several different sizes of these locks still in existence. Extend the tang as shown to engage the bolt in the lock. You will feel the bolt because it, too, is spring-loaded.

STANDARD HANDCUFFS

This next group of locks uses not only a barrel keyway configuration, but sometimes a flat ward is placed near the circumference of the center post—like the lock above—to prevent the turning of a rogue key. Some of the more expensive furniture barrel key locks use multiple

flat wards. A century ago, simple lever locks on shackles had no restrictions in the keyway and worked great. But prisoners got smarter and would use hard hedge thorns to pop their shackles. Later models of restraining shackles eventually incorporated the barrel key/ward concept used on furniture locks, which led to the next group: handcuffs.

To be able to pick open a pair of handcuffs is a very useful skill, to say the least. And unless you are handcuffed to a stationary object such as a radiator steam pipe and out of reach of any wire objects, you will now be able to slip out of any pair of cuffs in wide use today.

Figure 14 shows two methods to open these simple lever locks. Method 1 uses an L pick made from a large paper clip. If a crack, crevice, or hole is not available to bend the wire the 90 degrees needed to engage the lever tumbler, use the handcuffs" keyway to form the pick. But you must remember that the lever has to be held in place by the L pick while the shackle is pulled open. Figure 14 is a cutaway view of an old single-lever handcuff from a pair I bought at a gun store. I couldn't find a brand name or logo, and they appear to be at least 80 years old. But this gives you an example of the variety of handcuff-locking mechanisms still out there.

The other method to pop cuffs involves your local "hair stylist," the bobby pin. Open the bobby pin and scrape the plastic tip off the flat end. You can slip the flat side down the shackle clearance slot against the outer teeth of the cuff (as shown in Figure 14, method 2) and depress the paw lever directly, opening the handcuffs. You must hold the bobby pin against the paw-lever tumbler while pulling on the cuff to open it, or the cuff will lock again.

Police Handcuffs

I learned how to pick standard handcuffs as a kid but only recently had the opportunity to learn how to pop a pair of cop cuffs.

Figure 15 (image a) shows a direct template of a pair of stainless-steel Smith and Wesson handcuffs used by state and local police departments across America, After buying these from a gun dealer, I gave one cuff a good, old-fashioned autopsy (*de-engineered* is the technical term for this). They are laid out two-dimensionally at 85 percent of actual size, so

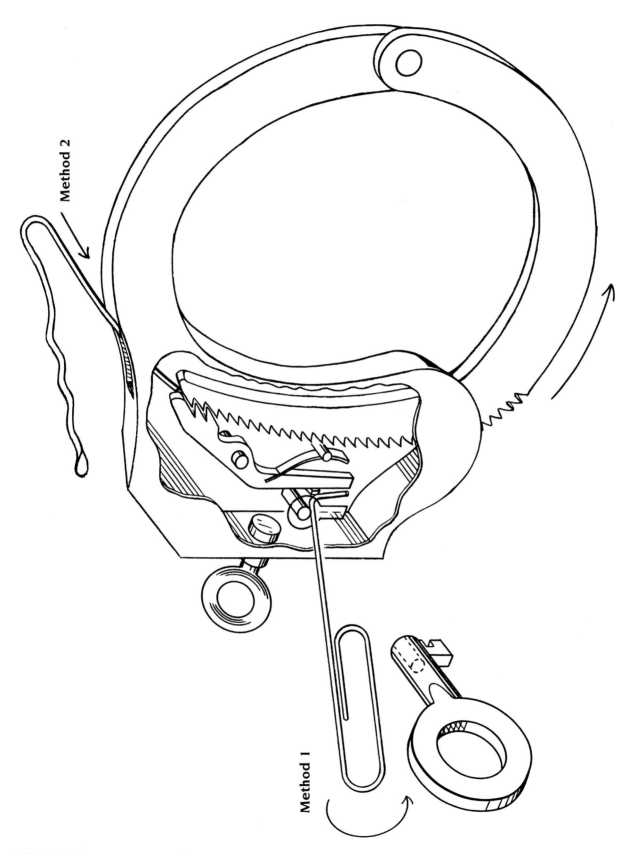

Method 2

Method 1

FIGURE 14
Standard handcuff (single lever, barrel ward).

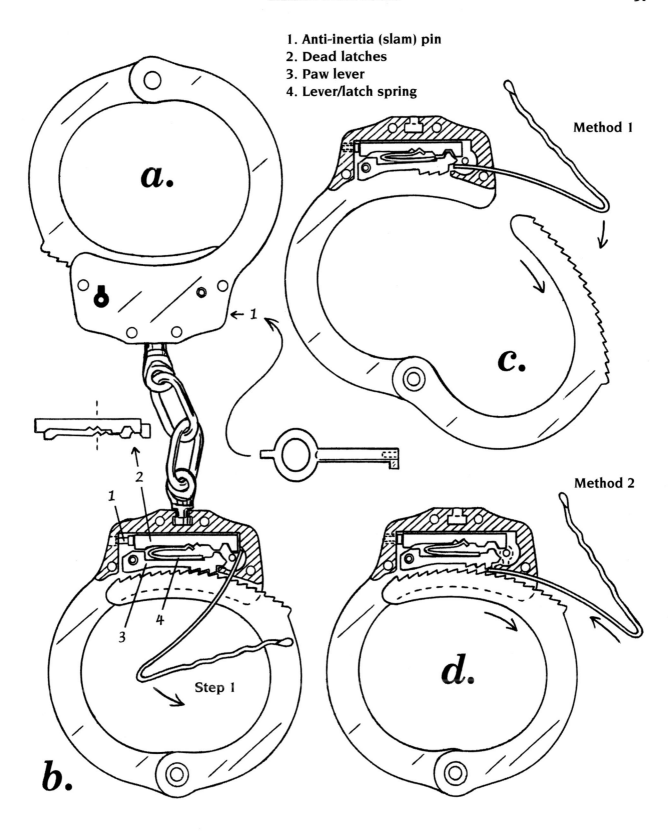

1. Anti-inertia (slam) pin
2. Dead latches
3. Paw lever
4. Lever/latch spring

Method 1

Method 2

Step 1

FIGURE 15
Police handcuffs (single lever, double dead latch, barrel ward).

On Smith and Wesson police handcuffs, one cuff had the rivets drilled to reveal the mechanism. This single-lever, double-dead-latch, barrel-ward lock can be picked opened with two different methods but requires that you first release the two dead latches.

that you may see the simple genius in its design. In fact, this simple lock could be technically classified as a single-lever, sequential (meaning the latches must first be actuated before the paw lever can be moved) dual-dead-bolt (these cuffs sport *two* parallel dead latches), warded (because of the barrel-key post) shackled lock. You can understand the difficulty I had in placing this lock in logical sequence in this book.

These modern handcuffs used by police departments have a set of dual dead latches (which move independently of each other) that are sandwiched together and must be released by the key (or proper picking action) to allow the paw lever to be moved (refer to Figure 15, image b). Most of the time, the anti-slam pin (1) that sets these two latches does not get pushed down with the end of the key when the cuffs are applied, so opening them is easy. Just use your L pick to depress the paw lever (3) through the key hole, retracting the teeth holding the cuff closed, and pull the bracelet open (image c). If the

latches (2) are pushed down, simply use the L pick to engage them, at the right of the keyway, and push them both up (image b). You can also do this by using the flat end of the bobby pin and running it all the way back into the keyway, to the back wall. Feel around to be sure that you have engaged both latches.

After opening both latches (step 1), you can then actuate the paw lever on the left of the keyway to open the cuffs (method 1, image c). If you are using a paper clip for your L pick, use a large one because a small one is not stiff enough to move the dual dead latches (2) against the force of the lever latch spring (4) and will bend on you.

The best wire tool for any handcuff is the dependable bobby pin. Being flat, it has the strength to do the above job *and* pick the lever (without having to be bent into an L shape), and to top it all off, it can be slipped into the cuff between the bracelet teeth and toothed paw lever (3) to open up the bracelet (method 2, image d). Such a versatile tool! Not many young girls use bobby pins nowadays, so they may not be as common as they once were; still, nearly all drug and department stores sell them.

The floating anti-slam pin (item 1) is there to prevent the dual latches (2) from being opened by slamming the cuffs against a hard surface, causing the momentum of the latches to slip past the spring (4) and fly down to release itself. It's based on simple physics (though probably discovered by accident) that the difference between the two objects (the pin and the latches) creates just enough inertial delay to prevent the heavier latches from flying freely open when the cuff is slammed against a hard surface (which would really smart but would release these dead latches without this pin).

Also note that it is relatively easy to pick the top latch, leaving the bottom latch locked. The anti-slam pin will snap up as if both latches are released; however, as you see in the latch detail—next to the cuff chain links—each latch sets itself on the lever latch spring (4) independently of each other (dashed line). A large paper clip will not engage both latches simultaneously, but because of its width a bobby pin will. You can still move both latches with a large paper clip, but you must do them one at a time. You can feel each one snap.

Another important note: If you buy a pair of used handcuffs, be sure to get at least two keys. Put one in a safe place because keys get lost. Put the other one on your primary key ring. Most of the time, you'll be lucky if you can get one key with a pair of used handcuffs. If this is the case, go directly to a locksmith for a set *immediately* after purchasing the handcuffs. For some odd reason, the smart juice drains out of the brain of some of the sanest people when handcuffs are around: someone inevitably winds up latched to somebody or something.

In any case, if someone does something dumb enough to get shackled with his hands behind his back, he might still be able to get out of the situation, provided he is limber enough to manage it, but he'd have to maneuver himself into a position to get his hands in front of him to pick the cuffs.

If that seems too difficult, then do what a heavyset friend of mine did: he mastered picking the cuffs with this hands behind his back (don't practice this one alone). This is referred to as the *blind method* or the *Houdini method*.

Chapter 8
FLAT-WARD LOCKS

Ward means to guard, as in "ward off." This word implies restriction, and when it comes to security, wards have guarded people's lives and valuables for almost a millennium.

Flat-ward door locks have been around for more than 700 years. The origins are hazy, but their ancient ancestors were used on doors in the churches of Europe. Christian monks often carried their huge, conspicuously ornate keys like scabbard swords, reassuring the masses that their church was safely secured behind the high-security of its warded locks. Now these locks are considered low-to-middle security, depending on the lock, and such fancy key bits can now be duplicated in any garage. But the descendants of these locks can now be found on

Replica of a traditional Tibetan warded key made by modern Tibetan refugee monks in Nepal. Original design circa early1700s from the Kham province of eastern Tibet and is based on an old Chinese lock, when trade reflected better relations between the two countries. Such keys were used by Buddhist abbots to enter monasteries and manage grain bins for the monks. The rope fob is durable hemp fiber, and the beads are campsite glass. As complicated as the 3-inch silver/brass key bit appears, a simple cam is turned 90 degrees at the end of a maze of five wards.

old house doors often with the classic old-style keyhole (shaped with a circle and triangle below it). This group of locks also includes the more recent (1920s on) Master Lock Company's laminated padlocks.

WARDED PADLOCKS

The most common warded padlock today is the Master laminated (meaning layers fastened together to form a stack; steel plates in this case) warded padlock. Still in wide use today, these locks sport case-hardened steel shackles, which repel hacksaw blade attacks, and they come in five basic sizes with varying shackle lengths on each: the tiny #9 (3/4 inch), #10 (1 inch), #22 (1 1/2 inches), #105 (1 1/8 inches), and the hefty #500 (1 3/4 inches) series. There are also older Master models that are no longer in production, such as the #209 series. There are a host of copycat products from other manufacturers, mostly from Hong Kong of the 1970s and 1980s and China of the 1990s, and nearly all have gone out of business. Slaymaker also made a line of laminated padlocks, but Master remains the master.

Back in the late 1960s and early 1970s, television commercials for the Master Lock Company would show one of its laminated padlocks being shot with a gun, leaving only a dent in the lock's side. I'm telling you, a bullet would only piss this lock off, possibly causing it to jam up even tighter. We are talking *layers of steel plate*, the thinnest point being about 1/8-inch thick. The shooter is more likely to damage himself from ricochet.

I recently watched a popular TV police detective show where the hero shot what looked like a laminated Master padlock on a warehouse door to save a fellow officer. It showed a dent in the lock's side as it recoiled from the assault, but the swinging shackle didn't mind and was still closed. The next scene was spliced in, and the padlock hung open: someone in the studio must have felt sorry for it and used the key. I was shocked that this cool TV cop would try picking a lock with a gun. I guess it's OK for the hero to shoot people on TV but not for him to actually pick a lock. The funny thing is that the detective was supposed to be quiet and sneak up on the bad guy in there working over his buddy. On top

of that, modern police departments have access to this information and can legally acquire lock picks. I know because a few of my other books are sold in the *National Police and Fireman's Catalog.*

Fortunately for locksmiths and cops, only two different pick key sizes (7/32- and 9/32-inch-wide bits) are needed to open all the warded version of these locks (including cheap copies of the Master warded laminated padlock still used in the United States and abroad).

In the upper left is the key (1) for the warded padlock shown (refer to Figure 16,). Compare the wards with the corresponding notches in the key. The zigzag keyway (or entrance) is also a ward of sorts, restricting entrance to the lock, but it rotates within the lock's housing. Below the key is a locksmith's pick key (2) used to open these

The #209 Master double-spring-lever, flat-ward padlock exposed. The rivets have been ground, punched out, and replaced with long screws and spacers to display the insides. Note hook-shaped retainer spring (item 6 in Figure 16), which also has to be picked to open this lock. The double-spring-lever (5) cannot be seen here and is on the far side of the retainer. The shackle spring (8) and entrance ward lie next to the lock.

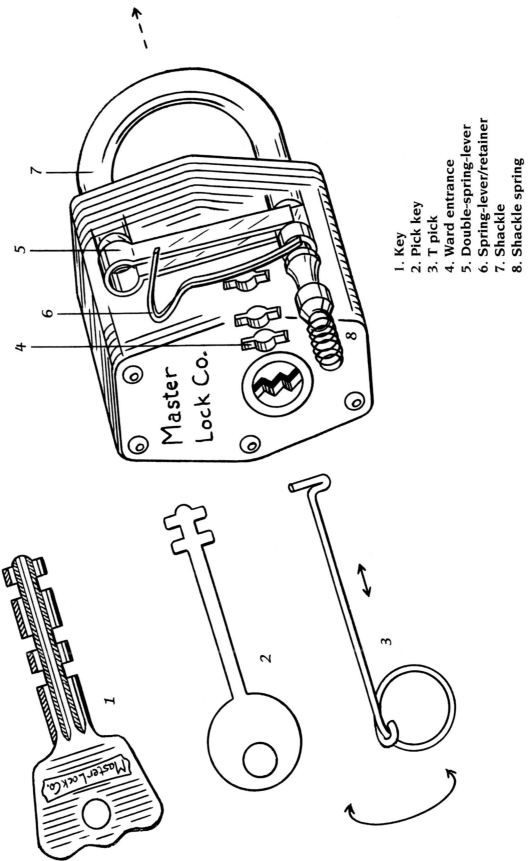

1. Key
2. Pick key
3. T pick
4. Ward entrance
5. Double-spring-lever
6. Spring-lever/retainer
7. Shackle
8. Shackle spring

FIGURE 16
Warded padlock (double spring-lever, flat ward).

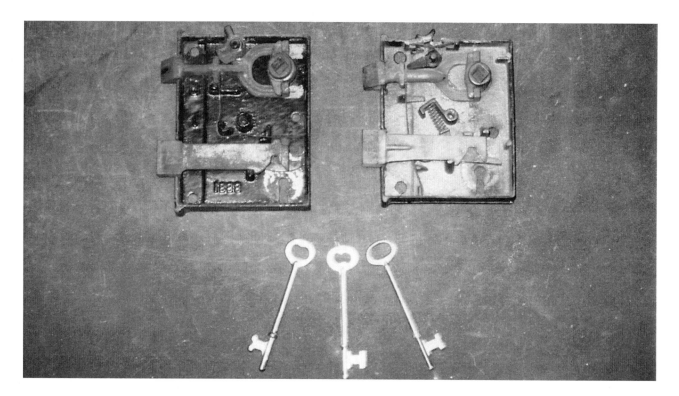

Two different warded house locks still in use in many older houses. The lock on the left was cast in 1888 and uses a single flat L spring for the whole works. The lock on the right was made later, circa 1900, when coil springs came into use. It employs two additional flat springs. The knobs are mounted on a spindle through a hub (item 7 in Figure 17). These locks are mounted on the inside surface of the door. Later warded house locks of the 1920s were mortised into the door. Below are three different passkeys that will open these venerable mechanisms.

two spring-lever warded locks. Below that is the homemade version, or the T pick (3). This tool will open this lock, provided you know how, which is the subject of the next topic.

To pick this lock, insert your T pick slowly, gently twisting it left and right. As you enter the lock, you'll sense "walls" or little "rooms" along the way. These stationary walls are called *wards* (4) because they divide chambers within the lock and prevent a flat piece of metal from simply being inserted and turned to open the lock. Here, each ward is a laminate plate.

Deep into the lock is a flat, heavy-gauge, hairpin-shaped spring that acts as a double-spring lever (5). It holds the shackle closed against the shackle spring (8)—cleverly disguised as a rivet. However, this "double-spring-lever" must be spread so that the shackle can be released.

If you can carefully place the end of your T pick between them, you can turn the pick, spreading this spring-lever, and pop the lock.

The larger #209 and #500 (illustrated in Figure 16) series Master padlocks use a second spring-lever retainer (6) and require a bit more skill to open. This second spring holds the shackle (7) onto the lock once the shackle is opened and allows the shackle to rotate or turn. But this retainer spring must be raised or spread like its daddy (5) above it before the lock can be opened.

Since the top spring-lever (5) is the widest, it must be picked first. Simply insert your T pick completely into the lock and gently twist it back and forth (about 30 degrees each direction) as you slowly pull the pick out of the lock. You will feel this main spring-lever as you spread it. When this happens, pull on the shackle (7) just enough to hold this spring open. Practice will tell you how much force is needed to pull the shackle—be firm but don't tug. Then, while holding the shackle, gently work your pick out (just about 1/8 inch) until you encounter the next springy-feeling lever—the spring-lever/retainer clip (6). Once you have twisted this clever boy, the shackle pops with a snap!

This lock can even be picked with a L pick but requires intermittent tugging on the shackle with skill, since the shackle has to be released occasionally. You may only spread one of the legs of the main spring-lever (5), and the other will hold up the picking of the retainer spring-lever. But the advantage to learning how to pop these locks with a L pick is that the tool is quickly and easily made without pliers.

Now, you may wonder whether a crowbar could pry the shackle open on this lock. It *might*, but believe it or not, if those two little springs become compressed edgewise (actually against three hardened surfaces) when the shackle is being forced, then you are just as likely to break the hasp on the door. This lock was designed for simplicity, efficiency, and *endurance*.

NOTE: The laminated padlock can also hold pin- and wafer-tumbler cylinders. Check the keyway to be sure of what is to be picked.

WARDED HOUSE LOCKS

These locks still grace the doors of many old farm houses in the Midwest and some of the grand old mansions of the South. Older wooden doors on homes and castles in Europe also have them, though they may have ornate lock and key designs—with some having up to four lever tumblers, or master-keyed with two keyholes—and are very difficult to pick. But here we'll only cover the most common warded house lock used

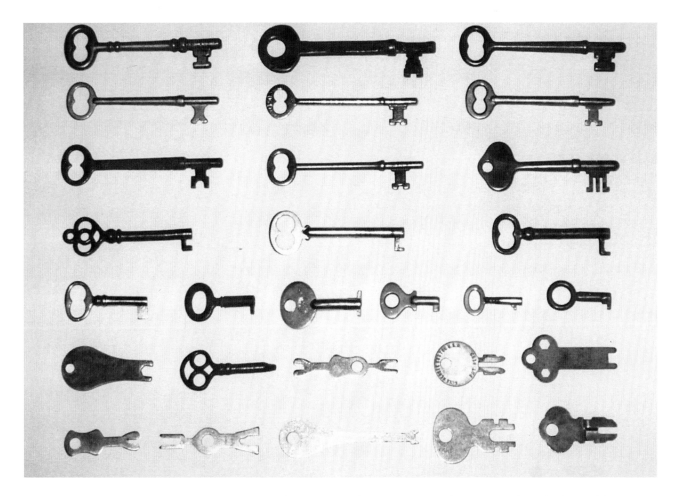

A collection of skeletons—keys, that is. From top to bottom: row 1 is standard coded ward house keys; rows 2 and 3 are warded house passkeys; rows 4 and 5 are barrel ward passkeys; row 5 is also a variety of handcuff keys; rows 6 and 7 are double-lever lock passkeys.

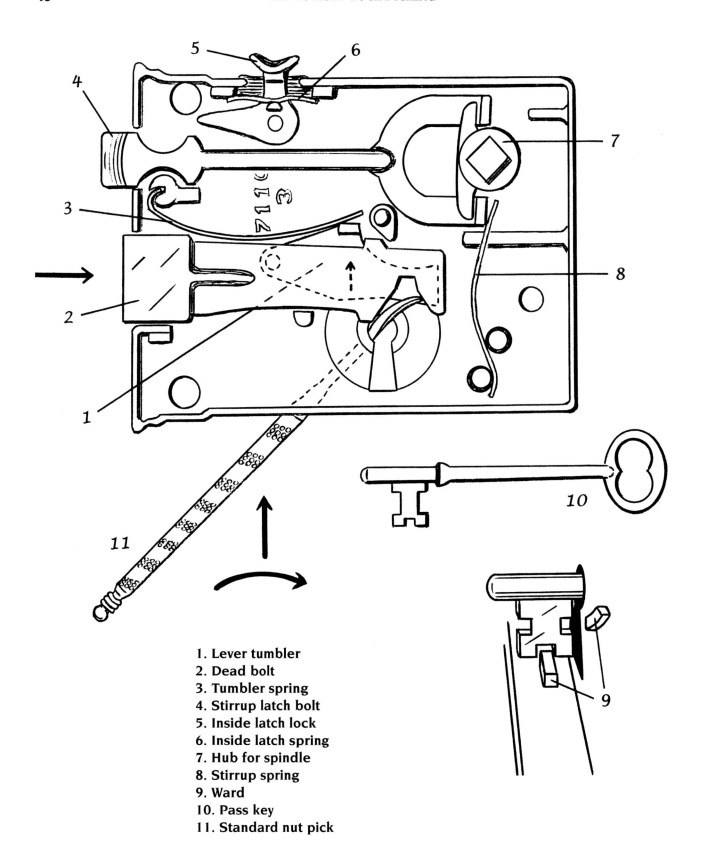

1. Lever tumbler
2. Dead bolt
3. Tumbler spring
4. Stirrup latch bolt
5. Inside latch lock
6. Inside latch spring
7. Hub for spindle
8. Stirrup spring
9. Ward
10. Pass key
11. Standard nut pick

FIGURE 17
Warded house lock (single lever, dead bolt, flat ward).

worldwide: the single-lever warded house lock.

Warded house lock keys are often called "skeleton" or "bit" keys (see Figure 17). Actually, a skeleton key is the cut-down bit key (10) that allows it *to pass the ward* (9) of all locks made in that style or group. This is the origin of the term *pass key*. Standard warded house keys look like the key bit shown passing the ward.

In Figure 17, the bolt (2) is "dead" because it cannot be pushed open by a knife blade (a common technique for a few centuries and now used on spring-loaded door latches) until the lever tumbler (1, dashed line) is raised—hence the term *dead bolt*. The "gate" (tab attached to the top of the tumbler and against the tumbler spring, item 3) will not allow the bolt to slide either open or locked until the lever tumbler (1) is raised.

Now, you may be wondering why this lock is not classified as a lever lock. Even though it does use levers to allow entry, the wards (9) provide the majority of security in this type of lock. Locks classified as lever locks usually have few if any obstacles to their levers and depend mainly on a multitude of levers that engage at varying degrees for their security. But most common warded house locks have only one lever.

In any case, even though this lock appears at first to be a cinch to pop, beware! You could find yourself picking a four-lever warded lock. Even with a collection of three dozen skeleton or pick keys, I still find myself having to occasionally pop an oddball warded house lock the hard way (with a pair of heavy-gauge steel welding wires— with flux removed—bent at awkward angles) for a customer. But in Figure 17 you can see how a single-lever warded house lock can be opened using a nut pick to lift the lever while also engaging the bolt.

If you cannot locate a nut pick, a wire coat hanger works, too. Unwrap the hanger and expand the hook part so that you can get it up into the keyway of the warded lock. Carefully rotate the hanger to engage the spring-loaded lever tumbler (1). (Be careful not to poke an eye with the wild, free end—it is best to shorten it by doubling the wire over and scissoring it back and forth to fatigue the bend, thus breaking the wire.) You will feel the lever tumbler (1) rise against its spring (3). While doing this, you can catch the dead bolt (2) at the top side of the keyway as well. While holding up the lever tumbler with the top side of the nut pick, slide the bolt back with the pick's tip. You will feel and hear the bolt slide open. The bolts on these locks must go left to open if the door has its hinges on the left, and to the right if the hinges are on the right. You can relock this lock by picking it in the opposite direction.

It's a good idea to visit your local locksmith and purchase a collection of various skeleton keys. They usually run between $1 and $5 each, depending on the lock and whether or not the key is antique and ornate. The only modern key maker of standard bit keys is Ilco/Unican, which carries 19 different styles of blanks, which have to be properly cut to work as pick keys. (If you feel ambitious, find out how to make your own professional locksmith pick keys in my books *Secrets of Lock Picking* and *Advanced Lock Picking Secrets*.)

Chapter 9
DOUBLE-LEVER DEAD-BOLT LOCK

Yup, you guessed it. If a single-lever dead bolt lock has worked for all these years, why not use *two* levers with a dead bolt? Although this lock has been around for almost 100 years, it is because this lock has teeth, which makes it a real bear to pick. I'd almost rather be faced with a high-security Medeco pin tumbler than to have to pick one of these in a hurry. But it can be done if you stay in practice. This is why I left this lock for last:

WOODEN DESK DRAWER AND MAILBOX LOCK

This furniture or desk lock uses two levers that must be aligned to allow the dead bolt to be retracted. This lock is also used on steel lockers and old-style post office mailboxes—but it is not recommended that you play with functioning mailboxes. That is a federal offense, and the postmaster general frowns upon such mischief.

These locks were made primarily by the Rockford Manufacturing Company, which is no longer in business, but the locks are still out there. The Belwith Company is the only current manufacturer of this lock.

In Figure 18, the bolt (2) in these locks is driven by the key (9) once it has aligned the lever tumblers (6). The bolt is also dead when unlocked because the lever's gates (4) will latch onto the bolt's racking stump (3; rectangular peg on the bolt) when it is retracted. The gates are the vertical slots in the levers. Note that the gates in the levers have teeth at their openings to snag the racking stump (3), mounted on the dead bolt (2), if any one of the lever tumblers (6)

does not quite line up with the gates. Also note that the bottom of the racking stump has a notch to snag inconveniently on the lever's teeth at the gate.

Of the locks in this book, this one is probably the most difficult to pick because the levers are essentially "invisible" to attempts to locate them. Also, the gates cannot rub up against the racking stump to give the lock picker feedback about how he is doing during the picking process.

In most cylinder locks you can feel when a tumbler is aligned. This is not so with this type of lock because the tumblers are "isolated" by the teeth at the gates (sounds like a B-rated horror movie), which snag when the bolt is being retracted by your Z pick (8). But this lock can also be readily picked with enough practice. Let's see how it's done.

First, you need to make a G pick (7) and a Z pick (8) from a standard paper clip. The business end of the Z pick should only be 3/16-inch long and made from a medium or large paper clip. The action end of the G pick should only be 1/8-inch long and formed from a small or medium paper clip. Now, insert the Z pick (8) all the way back into the lock until it stops. Then slowly rotate it clockwise until you feel the notch in the bolt and hold the tool there. Now insert the G pick (7) and feel for the spring-loaded lever tumblers (6).

When picking this lock, keep a constant but light pressure on the bolt with your Z pick. If you snag the racking stump, you'll have to ease off on the bolt, raise it, and try again. Since you can't see into the lock, it is a trial-and-error ordeal. You will have good results if you

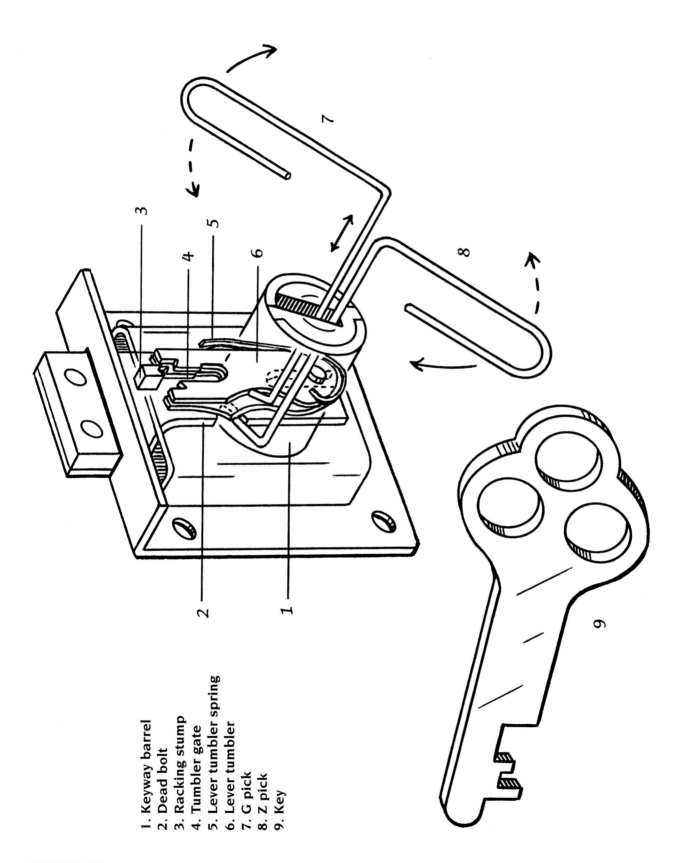

1. Keyway barrel
2. Dead bolt
3. Racking stump
4. Tumbler gate
5. Lever tumbler spring
6. Lever tumbler
7. G pick
8. Z pick
9. Key

FIGURE 18
Wooden desk drawer/mailbox (double toothed lever, dead bolt)

remember not to move the levers very far. The G pick on the right in the illustration has to engage only one lever at a time, so this simple two-tumbler lock could involve a fair amount of pick time. Again, with practice you can pop one within a minute—or even less with good karma.

Note that desk and furniture drawer locks sometimes house standard pin- or wafer-tumbler cylinders (which, as far as I'm concerned, are easier to pick) and yet are classified as providing higher security.

It should be noted here that key variation is low with these locks, meaning that there are only about 20 possible different keys that can be cut to open a two-lever lock such as this. In the eyes of the locksmithing community at large and the majority of lock makers, this means low security. But not many of these people have ever tried to pick one of these locks either. Here, the terms *pick resistance* and *security* can part ways. But the fact remains that flat-tumbler lever locks can cause premature hair loss.

Some lever locks use three to six levers with a dead bolt. These are used on older gym lockers, old lockboxes, and safe-deposit boxes. The last item typically uses two of the six tumbler locks and requires two keys to open the box. These locks are considered "high-security flat-tumbler locks."

Chapter 10
ELECTRONIC LOCKS

Security is only as good as the complexity of the system, and with electronic locks this is particularly so. Take, for example, card-reading systems. Most places of employment have card reader systems that not only allow the employees through the door but also log in the time that they enter and leave the place of business. This is also a most dependable way to keep track of who goes where.

These kinds of cards have a magnetic strip with encoded information along the bottom back side of the card. (You can see such strips on credit and debit cards.) This magnetic recording system uses data bits, which can only be in two polarized states—north/south, on/off, or 1/0. This is the *binary system* (meaning a system using two units), the language all digital computers read. For example, a simple three-letter word might read 011001101: 1 = on, and 0 = off. There can be a huge series of these magnetic north/south states (or in the case of computer circuits, electrical on/off states) in an immense variety of possible combinations. These magnetic states are called *domains*. This is the principle on which computer storage systems work, and a lot of information can be packed into a small amount of space such as on disks, either magnetic floppy, magnetic hard drive, or optical CD-ROM.

The act of swiping the card through a reader slot passes the series of domains, or data, one section at a time across a soft-iron core, which is wrapped with an insulated-copper-wire coil (see Diagram 1). This arrangement is called the *reader head assembly*, aka the "pickup head" in audio reproduction electronics.

Passing minute magnetic fields across the soft-iron core of this head induces a small electric current in the copper wire coil, which becomes a series of tiny electrical pulses that are amplified and sent out to the central processing unit (CPU). Here the signal is compared with already-programmed profiles in the erasable programmable memory (e-prom) chip circuits that the employer sets up by programming through the keyboard when the employee is hired. Quartz crystal oscillator circuits, or "clocks," establish time and the sequencing of events, and other circuits identify such employee criteria as department and shift, and logs this activity into memory. If everything jibes, the signal is accepted "at the gate" of a triggering circuit, which sends out a pulse to a buffer circuit, where it is isolated from outside shorting. The pulse is also increased in width (longer in time) when it makes it to the SSR, which controls 110 volts alternating current that drives the solenoid door bolt to release it from the doorjamb strike plate, allowing the door to be opened.

The card strip is magnetic, so care is needed to not erase the data by accidentally passing the card near a magnetic field, which could either reverse the polarity of the magnetic domains in the strip or wipe them out completely.

Because the system requires a complex array of signals to the input to operate properly, bypassing it requires some ingenuity. The modern card reader systems cannot be merely bombarded with random data to pop them like the electronic lock pick I described in *Advanced Lock Picking Secrets*. Electronic card readers have become much more sophisticated in the past

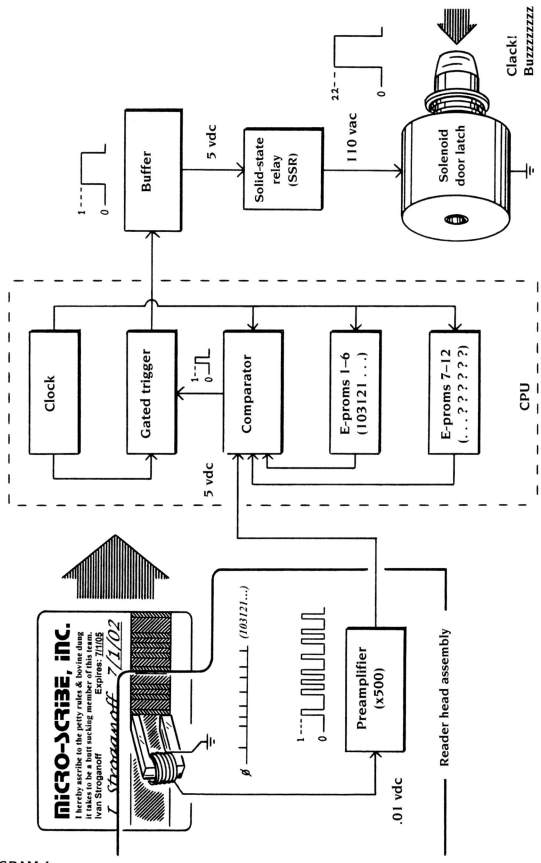

DIAGRAM 1
Magnetic card reader (electronic flow chart).

The Gemii Magnetic padlock with smoked Plexiglas panel installed by the author.

decade. But some of the older ones are still being used in many established factories here in the nation. Many foreign countries in the industrial world, as well, are also currently using these older models, and we'll see how to make a pick gun to open them. Also, the latest American entry systems use laser bar code readers like you see at grocery and department stores. Free enterprise nurtures new technology. However, these and the latest magnetic card reader systems are beyond the scope of this volume and may be covered in more detail in a later publication. But I mention them here because they operate on the principle of the simple magnetic padlock.

MAGNETIC PADLOCKS

On page 46 of *Secrets of Lock Picking* I show how a simple magnetic padlock works. This lock is a monopole type that works on the principle

that like magnetic poles repel each other, thus pushing the latch away from the shackle and opening the lock when the proper magnetic fields present themselves. It is the simplest type of magnetic lock.

However some magnetic padlocks are dipole. They use opposite magnetic poles that attract, as shown below in Figure 19. This type of magnetic padlock is a bit more complex, using an isolated latch plate between the tumblers and bolt or shackle.

Our sample lock here is made by Gemii. This lock is considered as upper low security, since there are only 16 possible key code changes (four pins to the second power of either north or south poles). However, it is of good upper low security, and if you don't have a pair of bolt cutters (or don't know what you are doing) it can keep you locked out.

The body is made of die-cast aluminum alloy—usually a standard brew of aluminum, zinc, and various other trace metals to make the material strong and lightweight. I used to work in a foundry that made lawnmower crankcases with this stuff. I also ran some of the machining operations to produce the final crankcase, and I can assure you that this stuff is tough! For this application it is great because these alloyed metals are also nonferrous (nonmagnetic). When I tried to de-engineer my sample lock, I assumed that it was of a ferrous material and couldn't figure out how it could use magnetics to function. The reason? A magnet would stick to its side (later I remembered that the steel shackle housed inside liked magnets). I also assumed this because the case was electroplated with a chrome finish.

However, the aluminum-zinc alloy making up the case gums up tools without an alcohol-and-water-based machining fluid. This is diabolical stuff; it accumulates heat (energy) rapidly. The mad-hammer approach would make the lock a mess, but you'd still be locked out.

Note that there are no openings in the lock. Even when unlocked, the shackle gives no clues as to how the sucker stays shut: there are no cuts or gaps on its end. With the lock opened, the shackle-end hole in the body is a dead-end hole, unlike with most padlocks where you can peek inside to see some guts. This hole is completely closed. There are no rivet indentations in the case sides, assembly cracks, or marks of any kind. Ultraviolet light gives no clues whatsoever.

I just had to get inside this lock. But it took me 3 days to figure out how to open it without destroying it and another 5 days to carefully draw it out on paper. The little monster was press-fitted with a peg-in-hole recessed panel (pegs and holes not shown in drawing). I had to use a Dremel cut-off wheel to edge out the panel and pry it out with a screwdriver, breaking off half the pegs.

When I did get the side off, my first thought was, "What a cheesy box of noodles—where's the meat?" (This lock was designed in America but made in Taiwan in the early 1980s, but I had no U.S. patent number and thus had to play coroner. It's probably no longer in production, but I have run across three of them in the past 5 years.) But the lock works and quite well. Now I have the lock mounted with a smoked Plexiglas panel in its side to safely display its innards with its key ball-chained to the shackle—a trophy for my

The Gemii magnetic padlock, locked with panel removed.

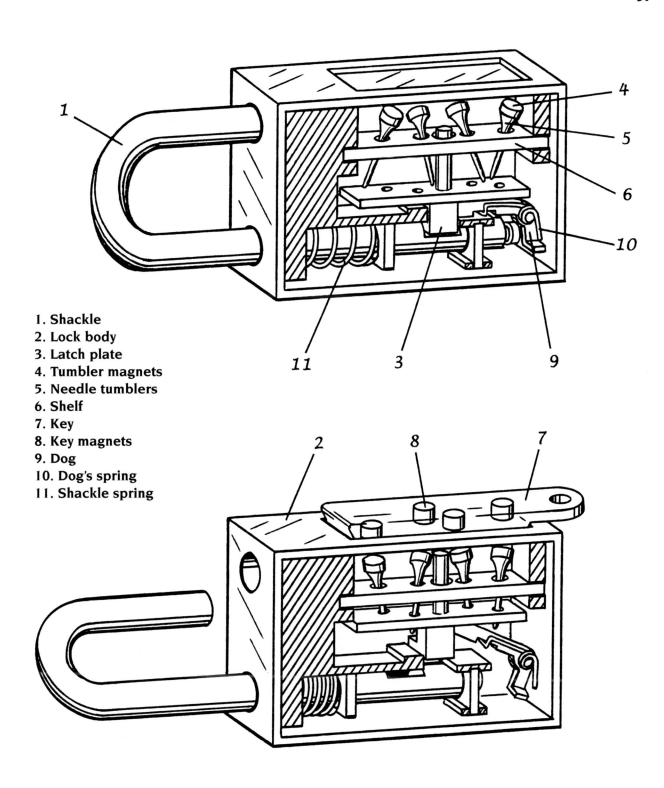

1. Shackle
2. Lock body
3. Latch plate
4. Tumbler magnets
5. Needle tumblers
6. Shelf
7. Key
8. Key magnets
9. Dog
10. Dog's spring
11. Shackle spring

FIGURE 19
Magnetic padlock (polarized needle tumbler, dead latch).

efforts to dissect the lock without tearing it up.

Anyway, my headaches are your gain, since Figure 19 shows how it works. This is the simplest form of magnetic two-dimensional locks in which complex magnetic card readers are based.

DESCRIPTION OF OPERATION

The shackle (1) is held fast to the lock body (2) by the latch plate (3). The pins are tiny cylindrical magnets (4) attached to "needle tumblers" (5) that freely float in the shelf (6). When the proper key (7) is placed into the recessed area of the lock's side, its key magnets (8) are arranged to attract the pin magnets (4) in the lock. These are aligned with the holes in the latch plate (3), and when the shackle is pulled, the dog (9) pushes the latch plate with the force of the dog's spring (10) far enough to clear the shackle, thus releasing it. The shackle spring (11) works the opposite way from most other padlock shackle springs in that it contracts (extension type) to hold the shackle closed when it is aligned with the case hole.

A friend of mine (let's call him Wong Li Dunn) worked at a high-tech plant that used a card reader system for clocking employees in. It also allowed entry through a side door to the plant. Wong had read my books and was curious. Being an engineer, he knew that to open the card reader without a card, he had to match the baud rate (the speed at which data are entered in this case, or the average rate that a card is swiped through a reader slot) to the security CPU. He also knew that he could only imitate the required magnetic data needed to allow entry: data needed to log in, such as badge number, wouldn't be read. So one day, he brought a battery pack and direct-current (DC) motor with a magnet attached to work with him. After several seconds of stroking the lock with his rotating magnetic "lock pick," it opened. But it wreaked havoc with the card reader system, and the payroll really got messed up. He bragged about his "Alexander Mundy" (the cat burglar in the It Takes a Thief TV show) invention to his co-workers, and the word spread to upper management. They too were very impressed, and Wong's last paycheck was for $0, and he was fired.

In Advanced Lock Picking Secrets, I demonstrated how to open magnetic padlocks and card locks

The Gemii magnetic padlock, opened with key.

with a few different electrically powered magnetic pick guns. Wong had not only discovered an easier and faster way to open older magnetic card readers, but unwittingly how to pop magnetic padlocks as well—even the isolated dipole padlock!

WONG LI DUNN'S MAGNETIC PICK GUN

Dunn used a battery pack and small DC motor for his magnetic pick gun, but we can simplify the works to make it very portable and convenient. The "armature" or rotating magnet should be made fairly accurate or the system will vibrate in the hand, causing the pick gun to bounce up and down. Also, such vibrations cause hand fatigue, not to mention possible nicking of the lock, thus arousing suspicion.

This armature can be made from a block of Delrin, nylon, ABS plastic, or aluminum. Don't use acrylic, Plexiglas, steel, iron, or any other ferrous metal. I made mine from a section of oak lathe. Hardwood is readily available in the required size, is nonmagnetic, and is easy to work.

Let's have some fun and build a magnetic pick gun. It requires a small rechargeable electric drill (variable speed is best). I used a $65 Makita 6041D nonvariable with a 450-rpm speed, and it worked fine. You may also opt for the really portable rechargeable screwdriver (refer to Figure 20).

You'll also need a block of oak or other hardwood measuring 1 x 2 x 1/2-inches thick. Usually wood lathe comes in 1 x 1/2-inch thick strips in varying lengths. Buy the minimum length, since you'll only need 2 inches. You'll need a 1/4 -20 flathead screw with nut and six pan-head wood screws size #6 (Phillips type is easiest to work with); they should be 3/8-inch longer than the width of the flat-bar magnet if you choose to use one. The magnet's poles (north, south) must be on its long ends, not on its face or sides. A magnet measuring 1 1/2 x 1/2 x 1/4-inches thick is ideal.

Step 1

Starting with the wood, cut off a 12-inch-long piece. With a pencil and square, mark off 2 inches from one end with a fine-point 0.5mm lead pencil. Do not saw it off just yet; the other 10 inches give you a handle to work with. Next, locate the center of the wood block by drawing an X across the 2-inch face from corner to corner (Figure 20, step 1). Lightly center-punch a mark with a small nail at this spot.

Here it is best to use a small drill press. But if you choose a hand-held electric drill, be very certain that you are drilling straight down. Check from two sides at 90 degrees apart to make sure the drill is not leaning. Use a 3/32-inch drill bit and drill a pilot hole clean through where the X crosshairs meet. This is center.

Step 2

Next, locate your magnet over this block and, with a screw, rest it down along the magnet and lightly tap it, leaving a mark in the wood with its tip. For the system to work safely, you should have at least six marks, as illustrated in Figure 20, step 2. Center-punch with a nail and drill the six pilot holes clean through also with the 3/32-inch drill bit. Now redrill the center hole using a 15/32-inch bit. The large 1/4-20 x 1 1/4-inch flathead screw should turn down into the hole snug but not too tight. If you can't get the screw started (some 1/4-20 flathead screws vary in size), enlarge the center hole by drilling with a 1/4-inch bit. It is important that the screw be centered and snug—you don't want the tool to wobble.

Remove the flathead screw and countersink a V depression so that the 1/4-20 flathead screw will mount down flush to the top surface of the block with its head just below the wood's surface. You can use a 3/8-inch drill bit to carefully cut out this depression if you don't have a countersinking tool. Use caution, clamp the piece down firmly, and drill slowly at medium speed. Countersink a little bit, then check by inserting the flathead screw. Repeat this process until the flathead is just below the surface of the wood so that the magnet lies above it but flat against the wood's surface.

After all the pilot holes are drilled, you are ready to cut off the 2-inch end of the piece. This part was left for last, so you have a handle to hold while drilling. For hardwood, I have found that a hacksaw works just fine. If you are good with wood, however, and have a table or chop saw, you'll get a nice, clean cut. You can even sand and varnish the block if you wish.

Step 3

Now cut the corners from the block of wood

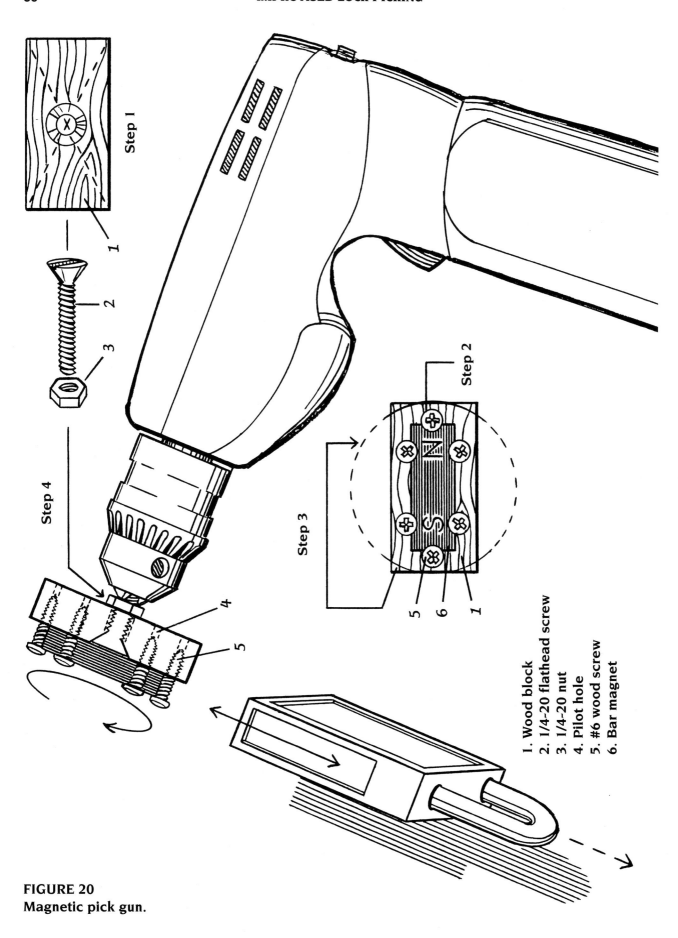

Step 1

Step 2

Step 3

Step 4

1. Wood block
2. 1/4-20 flathead screw
3. 1/4-20 nut
4. Pilot hole
5. #6 wood screw
6. Bar magnet

FIGURE 20
Magnetic pick gun.

using a coarse wheel grinder (this dirties the wheel), wood sander, or hacksaw. The corners should be cut at the arc of a 2-inch circle. Use a 2-inch-diameter lid from a small jar as a template and mark with your fine lead pencil.

Step 4

For final assembly, run the 1/4-20 flathead screw down into the block and tighten the 1/4-20 nut at the bottom. Turn it until it bites into the wood. If you can't find a 1 1/4 (1.25)-inch flathead screw, cut a 1 1/2-inch screw down to 1 1/4 inches. To do this, start by running the nut up the top of the bolt and carefully cut off 1/4 inch from its end with a hacksaw or cut-off wheel. Next remove the nut. This helps to clean the threads on the tip of the bolt. Then lightly file with a fine-steel file to remove sharp edges; this end is exposed when the block is not in the drill's chuck and could snag on clothing or skin.

Now mount your flat-bar magnet and clamp it down with the #6 pan-head wood screws at the six spots into the block, as shown in the illustration. Be certain that the magnet is centered and the screws are evenly placed, or, again, you'll have unwanted vibration that could also make the tool rock in your hand, bumping and nicking the lock you are so diligently trying to open.

Optimal Baud Rate

Using Wong's rotating magnetic field I was able to pop the Gemii magnetic padlock. First, I used a 110-volt drill plugged into a Variac (adjustable voltage source) so that I could increase or decrease the speed of the spinning magnet. I discovered that 300 rpm works best for these padlocks. This equates to about two-thirds of the top drill speed of the Makita. Our home-made magnetic pick gun with the Makita drill also works but takes a few seconds longer. These magnetic pick guns set up an oscillation of the lock's four magnets by first repelling and then attracting each magnet (no matter the polarity of the configuration) and causes it to vibrate at approximately 2.5 Hertz or cycles per second.

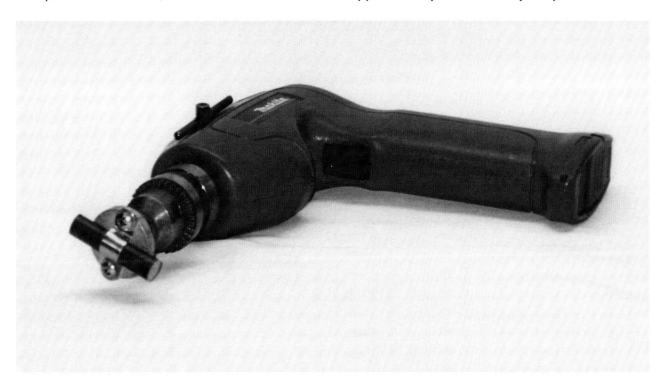

The Wong Li Dunn magnetic pick gun for opening a wide variety of magnetic locks and older card readers. Here is Wong's original armature, which came out of a Thermolyne chemical stirrer used in research and university labs. The spinning magnet magnetically links with another rod magnet placed inside a beaker containing the liquid that is to be stirred. The same principle is used in decorative liquid "tornado" lamps.

With intermittent tugging of the shackle, and the stroking of the running magnetic pick gun across the lock's magnets, the lock pops open within seconds every time. It doesn't matter which direction the armature spins, forward or reverse.

WARNING: Always keep your face clear of spinning magnetic armature and always wear safety glasses!

Chapter 11
COMBINATION DISK LOCKS

In the 1850s Linus Yale Jr. invented the modern safe lock, which allowed people to securely stash their treasures. But along with the improved lock came the safecracker.

The premise of the disk safe lock is simple (refer to Figure 21, image b), but when it was invented 150 years ago, it was considered pure genius. Let's look at the simplest disk combination lock, the common padlock.

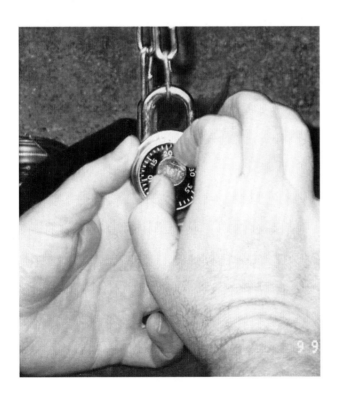

Free-handing the classic #1500 Master combination padlock. Practice with S hooks and a bicycle chain to hold the lock.

A driver disk (2) is attached to the dial (1) through the front of the lock's casing. It has a peg protruding from its surface, which engages a second disk (3) with its own peg (4) when turned. The second disk is mounted to the back wall of the lock on a spring-loaded shaft. The second disk also has another peg to engage the last disk (5) behind it on this shaft. All disks have a notch cut out somewhere about their circumference. This notch is called the *gate* (6). This arrangement allows the dial to set any one of these disks to line up their gates to a bolt using the proper code. The bolt in turn drops into the tumbler gates to allow the latch (in this case the padlock's shackle) to be pulled open. Now let's look at the combination padlock in more detail and figure out how to open it without its code.

MODEL #1500 MASTER
COMBINATION PADLOCK

The world's most popular combination padlock, the classic Master #1500 series combination padlock (Figure 21, image a), has endured the test of time. This lock has fewer parts than most other padlocks, yet for more than 4 decades it has continued to keep the casual thief locked out. Only a handful of skilled locksmiths can manipulate these locks open in less than 5 minutes. Three simple disks can be set to three sets of numbers with 1,500 possible combinations. You have a 1-in-1,500 chance of dialing out the right code the first time. Basically this is a puzzle lock, and if you like puzzles, it's a good one.

This lock introduced me to safes; it was used

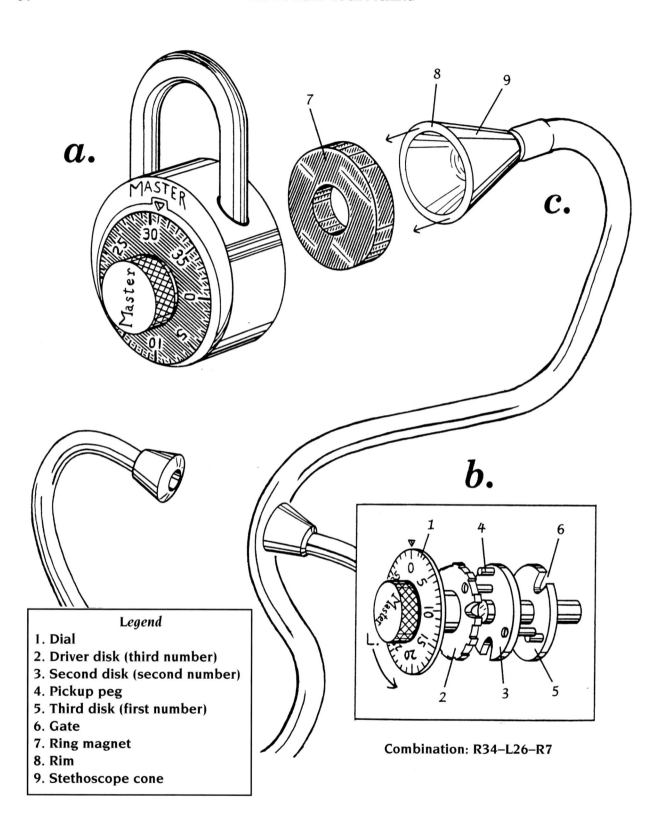

a.

c.

b.

Legend
1. Dial
2. Driver disk (third number)
3. Second disk (second number)
4. Pickup peg
5. Third disk (first number)
6. Gate
7. Ring magnet
8. Rim
9. Stethoscope cone

Combination: R34–L26–R7

FIGURE 21
Safe-o-scope.

exclusively in my high school locker room. After getting pretty good with opening this lock, I had little trouble with other combination locks, from two-disk piggy banks to an old four-disk Sargent & Greenleaf safe. Its small size and design make this lock ideal for beginning safecrackers to practice on.

Free-Handing

When opening any combination lock, you must first "clear" the tumblers (that is, turn the dial three to four full revolutions clockwise (most combination locks start their code going right). Now, if you place your ear to the back of the lock and slowly turn the dial to the left, you'll hear clicks. Do not pull down on the shackle while doing this. These clicks are the pegs engaging each other in turn as you rotate the dial. The front disk turns and picks up the middle disk. The middle disk in turn picks up the back disk.

The first step to free-handing combination locks: identify and catalog your combination lock collection. Write the combination, serial number, and date when you first opened the lock on a key tag. By identifying each lock, you can associate the sound of each disk/bolt encounter.

The trick to opening the Master #1500 is simple. I discovered that if you happen upon the first number, you can locate the second number and that the third number is free. So in 40 tries you should have it opened. But finding that first disk alignment is difficult in the newer Master combination padlocks because you can no longer hear the first tumbler by dragging it across the bolt's tongue. It and the second tumbler are slightly smaller than the serrated driver disk attached to the dial. But if you can align the first disk and pull on the shackle, the bolt rubs past that tumbler's gate and eases the shackle a bit, telling you the first code number.

In Figure 21, image c you see a homemade safe stethoscope. This device helps to hear the subtle sounds made by disk tumblers as they are picked up by neighboring disks. Not counting the dial's disk tumbler, for every one of these clicks, add a tumbler. If you get two light clicks while clearing the tumblers there are three disks in the lock. If you hear three clicks, there are four disk tumblers in the lock and chances are you're playing with a safe.

The stethoscope also allows you to easily view the dial while working the code and tells you when each disk's gate loses its ringing sound when aligned with the bolt. As the shackle is being pulled, the bolt drops down upon the tumbler stack and lightly kisses the disks. If its sound has dropped in volume and pitch, the number under the arrow on the dial face is one of the combination numbers in the direction that you are turning the dial. Write that number down on paper.

Now turn the dial left one complete turn and you'll hear its peg pick up the peg of the second disk. The moment this happens, pull firmly down on the shackle and release it on every other number. For example, should the second disk pick up at 15, then pull down on the shackle on 17, 19, 21, and so on until you hear the hollow sound of its gate. That is your second code number. Jot that down as well.

Finally, the last number of the code is on the dial itself, attached to the last disk with those noisy bumps on its circumference. Turn the dial right. Do the same as above, but counting backward. For example, each shackle pull could be on 3, 1, 39, 37, and so on until the shackle pops right open. Just as well write that one down too and have the whole combination recorded. While I have my pen out, I also jot down the lock's serial number (stamped across the padlock's back) next to the combination. In this way each lock in my collection has an identity. I still like to practice on them occasionally without looking up their codes.

These locks are serial-numbered to a codebook that reveals the combination of all Master padlocks manufactured in the past 40 plus years. For example, you could look up serial number 584102 stamped on the back of my gym locker's Master combination padlock and find the combination to be 2–17–34. The number assignment is randomly generated by computer, and there is no way to decipher the code without the codebook, which not surprisingly is not handed out freely. There is a new edition of the publication each year because each batch of new padlocks manufactured has different codes. In any case only 1,500 combinations are used.

In *Secrets of Lock Picking*, I pointed out how to open these locks by smacking them at a certain spot with a hard *rubber* mallet to open them. This technique has to be performed precisely and thus is not always successful. This often leads to a severely beaten padlock still hanging from its hasp, taunting the attacker and more stubborn then ever. It's also more difficult to manipulate this lock open if it has been struck along its side, since this tightens the stainless-steel jacket against the shackle and binds it. Sometimes you can solve this problem with a pair of Channellock pliers by gripping the padlock's body from top to bottom in the pliers' jaws and squeezing the casing back to round.

How to Make a Locksmith's Stethoscope
Medical stethoscopes are available through college bookstores, which furnish supplies to students in nursing courses. They cost about $25 and come with vinyl tubing in different colors and basic black. If you don't have a community college or medical college in your area, try a medical supply store. Any town with a hospital usually has one, but you'll probably have to pay more for the stethoscope.

A flat diaphragm-style stethoscope will work, but try to find the older style cone type, which amplifies the sound better when glued to a ring magnet and is also cheaper. Hobby and craft

stores carry flat ring magnets. Try to get one that's 1 inch in diameter with at least a 1/4-inch hole (1/2 inch is better) in the center. If you do purchase a diaphragm type, find a magnet with a larger hole to give the diaphragm free clearance. The magnetron of an old, small microwave oven works quite well. Magnetrons have two bad-boy ceramic magnets that create a magnetic "bottle" for the microwaves. Just be careful not to slam these powerful magnets together because they are quite brittle and break easily. The thickness of a store-bought ring magnet doesn't matter too much, but it should be strong enough to hold firmly to a refrigerator door. If all else fails, check Radio Shack, which carries flat ring magnets.

Now, attach the magnet to the stethoscope (Figure 21, image c). Remove the cone from the tubing of the stethoscope and set aside. I use DAP brand silicone adhesive made by Dow Corning to bond the two. I've used this glue on the Pyrex glass of a 400-degree convection oven, which was actually a large glass pot. This stuff is tough. It comes in a 1-ounce tube on a card from ACE Hardware stores. Use rubbing alcohol to clean the ring magnet (7) and cone (9) to be glued and dry with a clean paper towel. Apply a narrow beaded ring about 1/16-inch wide on the outer rim of the stethoscope cone's rim (8). Position the cone directly over the magnet and gently push flush with the magnet. Carefully check the position and try not to slide it around, for this will pile glue along one side of the inner section of the cone, possibly plugging the auditory canal of the bell. Let it stand undisturbed for a full 24 hours. Once set, the magnet and cone will be difficult to separate.

You can now attach your "safe-o-scope" to the back of a Master combination padlock and hear everything going on inside. Also, you can face the dial and not have to think in mirror-image terms, so you see which direction you're turning the dial. You can use this scope to listen to anything mechanical, such as checking for bad bearings in electrical motors or bad valves in automobile engines.

Peeling a Practice Combination Padlock
These locks make certain sounds when being manipulated, but words cannot convey the likeness of the actual sounds themselves. You must expose the tumblers so that you can

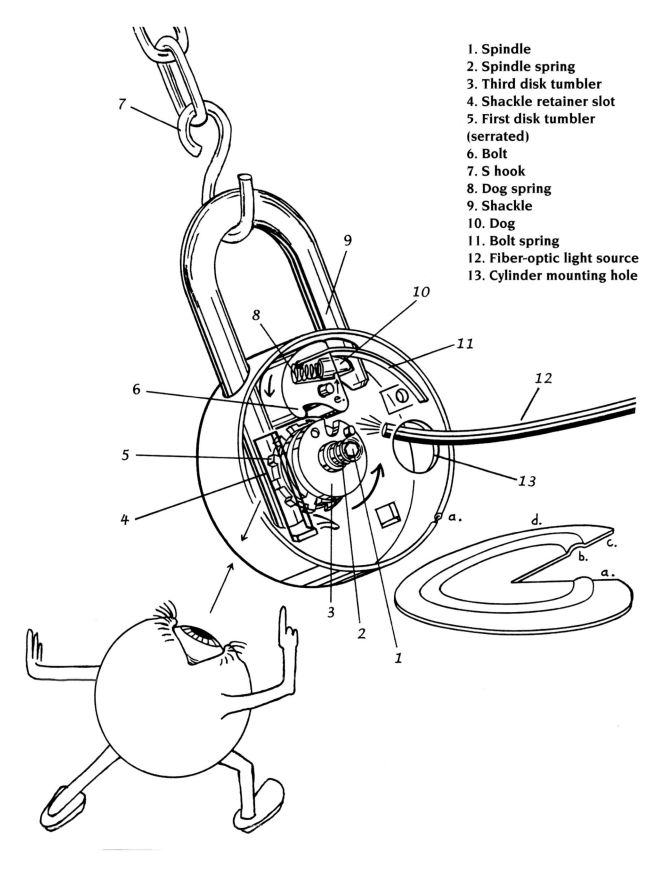

1. Spindle
2. Spindle spring
3. Third disk tumbler
4. Shackle retainer slot
5. First disk tumbler (serrated)
6. Bolt
7. S hook
8. Dog spring
9. Shackle
10. Dog
11. Bolt spring
12. Fiber-optic light source
13. Cylinder mounting hole

FIGURE 22
Combination padlock (triple disk, serrated isolation).

associate the sounds you hear with what the tumblers are doing.

You can simply remove the back stainless-steel jacket plate of the Master #1500 as easily as opening a tin can and peeking inside with a fiber-optic penlight to see the bolt and gate alignments (see Figure 22). A few moments of dialing and you're in.

To do this, peel the back from the lock, exposing the tumblers. Do this by first using a hacksaw to cut a thin groove from the lower, outer edge or rim of the padlock and saw to the center (a). Next, work the corner of the blade of a medium flat-blade screwdriver into raised ridge (b) and pry up until the back jacket edge is free (c) from the lock. Finally, work the screwdriver around with blade flat to back of lock, until you work the edge out (d) and the plate falls free.

CAUTION: Do not to impale yourself with the screwdriver; always force the tool away from hands, legs, face, or other body parts. A screwdriver can slip from the work piece and leave a deep, nasty gash. The most common injury is to the base of the thumb. It has lots of blood vessels, and bleeding may be very difficult to stop, so be careful.

Now, you may wonder, "If I have a hacksaw, why don't I just cut the shackle?" You *could* cut the shackle but not with a hacksaw. The shackle is case-hardened steel, and the blade won't even scratch it. A right-angle grinder or cut-off wheel will, but the purpose of this exercise is to have an intact, but exposed padlock to practice free-hand manipulation on. You could use this technique for entry and relock the padlock. Maybe someone wouldn't notice right away, but usually it's obvious.

Nite Ize (www.niteize.com) makes fiber-optic penlight adapters, which work great on a variety of Mini-Maglite flashlights. I wish I had had this tool a number of years ago when I was renting an old remodeled house (it had been a house of ill repute in the red light district about 80 years ago) that had something odd embedded in the wall of my roommate's closet. My roommate and I couldn't figure out what it was. At a glance, it looked like the end of a sewer vent pipe that had been capped off. One day while cleaning the closet after my roommate moved out, I noticed a hole dead center in this "drain cap." It had a machined vertical line right above it. This was a

A peeled Master combination padlock. By removing the back jacket from the lock and using a fiber-optic light source through the round cylinder mount hole, you can find the combination through the shackle retainer slot (near bottom of the lock in photo and item #4 in Figure 22). Note the hacksaw scoring mark located at around 5 o'clock.

wall safe that had been built into the original house frame. This sucker was anchored in for keeps. Someone must have knocked off the dial and punched the shaft. My heart raced. "I get to crack this baby in the privacy of my own house, and no one has to know!" I thought out loud.

I soldered a pair of insulated wires to a tiny DC lamp and ran it through the 1/2-inch hole. I then connected the leads to a battery pack. This illuminated the interior of the safe along with the back of the lock. I then cut a piece of mirrored Plexiglas (3/8 x 4 x 1/8 inches thick) and mounted it by using an extension spring on the end of a 10-32 threaded 3/16-inch-diameter flexible Delrin rod. This gave me a 4-inch-long spring-necked mirror that I could insert and push back against the inner back wall of the safe to see the back of the combination lock inside. I could also rotate the rod to make the mirror scan up or down, showing me the whole view of the back of the lock in 3/8-inch strips.

Peeping into the hole, I found why the safe door would not open. The three tumblers had fallen off to one side and lay against the bolt, preventing it from being retracted. Apparently, the knob was also the handle and pulled the door open, once the proper combination was dialed. I tried off and on for 3 months with a variety of homemade tools made from flux-stripped welding rods but couldn't catch any one of the tumblers to move it out of the way. Had I thought to use a fiber-optic light source, I could have drilled a hole in the right place and illuminated the area better, quite possibly finding a way to move the tumblers. The bolt would have been easy to throw then. In any case, using the mirror, the only object I could see lying on the antique carpeted floor of the safe was an equally antique wrench. Still, it would have been a real thrill to open it.

A fiber-optic penlight is a small but very

Master combination lock with back plate pried off after the casing lip had been ground away. Note the two disk tumblers (first two numbers dialed) mounted on the spring-loaded shaft to the back plate.

useful investment and allows you to see into keyholes of pin, wafer, and lever locks to count the tumblers. You also can identify the type of tumblers in a lock and, as with the next case, shed light on where the gate is in each disk tumbler.

Principle of Operation

The locking dog (Figure 22, item 10) and bolt (6) assembly are safely enclosed within the loop of the shackle (9), protected from one primary plane of attack: all about its circumference. The bolt occupies the most space in the lock, other than the shackle. The disk tumblers take up little space, so you may be surprised at all the empty space inside it. Yet, this lock remains a good value from generation to generation.

The serrated disk tumbler (5) depicted at the bottom of the stack (shown slightly exaggerated for easy viewing) is the last tumbler to be aligned in a successful opening. It is the easiest number to find, but unfortunately for a would-be thief it is the last number dialed. Aligning the other two tumblers' gates to the bolt is difficult because of the notches around the outer edge of this disk, and the disk is slightly larger than the other two disks. The bolt encounters this disk first, not touching the other two, isolating them from the bolt.

When working with these padlocks, either by manipulation or with the hacksaw, use a pair of 1 1/2-inch S hooks (7) and a lightweight bicycle chain to secure it to a stationary object. This is also how you secure the padlock for practice. Hold the padlock face down in one hand and pull firmly against the chain. The other hand can now safely cut a groove in the back jacket (Figure 22, action a) with the hacksaw. Install a new, fine-toothed blade in the hacksaw. Place the cut 145 degrees clockwise from the top of the padlock, or where the lower segment of the letter Q crosses the O. On the back of most of these padlocks, this spot is the "WI" of the stamped "Milwaukee, WI." Saw until you have a groove deep enough to open up area b.

The spindle (1) is swaged to the back case, holding the last two disk tumblers. It does not hold the dial, just the last two disks (the first two numbers dialed). The bottom serrated disk (5) is swaged to the dial, and the dial knob is hollow inside. So if you punch this spindle (1), you'll still be locked out.

With the back stainless-steel jacket plate removed, insert the fiber-optic end into the round auxiliary four-pin-tumbler cylinder mounting hole (13), and illuminate the spot right at the bolt's tongue (6). It's best to do this by shining the fiber-optic light source (12) just back of the third disk tumbler (3; the first number dialed) so that you illuminate the whole back disk tumbler's surface. The front tumbler is attached to the dial and is the last number dialed. So once you clear the tumblers right, look into the back vertical shackle retainer slot (4) on the left of the padlock's back and line up the third disk tumbler's gate to the tongue of the bolt (6). Stop and look at the front of the lock. Write down that number. Now, turn the dial one complete turn to the left and stop. Look into the back of the lock again and turn the dial (make sure you go left). The second or middle disk starts to turn. Stop when its gate also is aligned. Write that number down. Now turn the dial right until the last gate is aligned and write that number down. The shackle should pop open.

Spare Change

You may want to peel a second practice combination lock but do not deduce or otherwise discover its combination. When you hear a peculiar sound while working that combination lock, check in the back of the lock, as illustrated in Figure 22, and observe where the disk tumbler's gates are aligned. Remember that sound.

With daily practice, and after working on a few, you may find popping combination padlocks mere child's play. At first, it may take you thousands of free-hand dial turns. With continued practice on various combination padlocks, you can get good and may even occasionally free-hand one open in less then 30 seconds. It depends on your energy level at the time and how much practice you have under your belt. Visualize the inside of the lock with all its parts. This will help you to free-hand open most of the combination padlocks that you encounter.

Practice first on older padlocks and then work your way up to the newer ones. The older ones have a steel knurled dial knob swaged to the numbered steel dial face. Later models use a molded, one-piece, cast-aluminum-alloy dial.

Punching a Master: carefully punch a hole at 3:30 with a medium 1/4-inch shoulderless flat-blade screwdriver and mallet. (For safety reasons, read text first.)

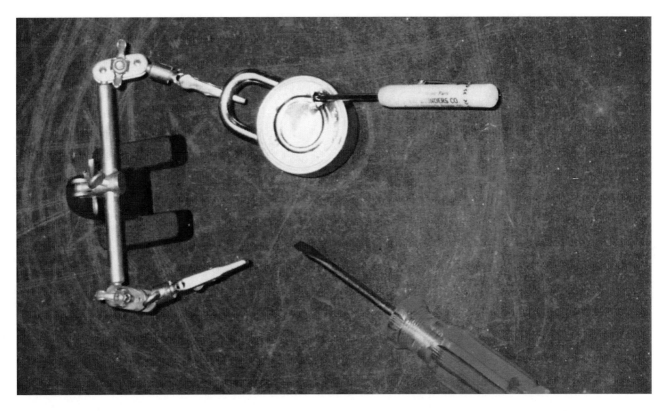

Depress the locking dog (Figure 22, item 10, area e) with a small screwdriver to open the combination padlock.

Tips on Fingertips

At the turn of the 20th century, some 50 years after Linus Yale Jr. invented the disk tumbler lock, safecrackers sanded their fingertips to increase their sensitivity for feeling the disk gates of a safe lock. In the movies of the 1940s and 1950s, you'd often see a guy in black and white doing this for the "big heist tonight." Well, safes have changed since then. Even though they use Yale's basic design, they are a lot tougher to open than those portrayed in those movies. And the fancy, whirly, knob-turning, blinkity lights, electronic black-box devices used in later movies to open safes are pure wishful thinking. In a recent movie, I was disappointed to see James Bond use an X-ray device to see into the lock, allowing him to line up the tumblers and open the safe. It takes no skill to use such a device (even if it were possible to see through hardened steel and exotic metal laminates). Effectively popping combination padlocks requires practical experience, common sense, and real-time practice.

You can sand your fingertips to make them sensitive to the tumblers of a Master combination padlock. For some people this helps, but I personally don't think it's necessary. However, if you do find that it helps, remember this: eventually the tips will become calloused, demanding more sanding, and if you practice regularly, you must make it a routine to keep them sanded. So for beginners, it's best not to sand your fingertips unless they get calloused from all the practice on these locks. They will be tender and sensitive anyway from using them regularly.

Punching a Master

If you're in a big hurry, you can simply rape the lock. Some Master combination padlocks come with an optional four-pin-tumbler brass cylinder in the back. In this way, a group of locks can be master-keyed to one key holder. The gap at the bottom of the locking dog (Figure 22, item 10, area e) is where the end of the cylinder's cam rests, which will depress this dog once the cylinder is turned. You could pick this lock, but the pins are tiny and require special picks (see *Secrets of Lock Picking* and *Modern High-Security Locks* for more information on picking small pin-tumbler cylinders). If the Master combination padlock does not have this auxiliary pin-tumbler cylinder in its back, you can "punch" the lock.

On an unpeeled Master combination padlock, locate on the back the area where it is stamped "Made in USA." If the back were a clock, this spot would be at 3:30 and between the outer rim of the lock and the circular ridge (Figure 22, area b). With a medium 1/4-inch shoulderless flat-blade screwdriver, locate this spot and punch right through using a mallet or the handle of a larger flat-blade screwdriver if you have no

mallet. Wear safety glasses and don't punch your hand. Once you have broken through the thin stainless-steel jacket, use the medium screwdriver blade to open the hole completely, carefully using a twisting and prying motion.

Next, push down on the shackle and run the pocket screwdriver blade up through the pin-tumbler mounting hole (Figure 22, item 13). Place its tip against the end of the dog (10e.) and depress the dog. This releases the shackle.

This inherent weakness, once exposed, would make the lock extinct and our knowledge of it useless. Like the virus that destroys its host, it dies too. So let's keep this last technique just between us locksmiths, OK?

CONCLUSION

For locks using more than two levers (or three discs) that engage a bolt, the security escalates. Ironically, the more complex a three-dimensional mechanical lock gets, the easier it can be to open—if you know how and you practice opening it.

FLAT-TUMBLER LOCKS

As you can see by our encounter with the last few locks, the flatter the tumblers, the tougher they are to pick. But in the world of security, "tumbler" implies variation, and in the past flat tumblers have *not* been able to provide as much variation as more dimensional systems. Generally it is accepted (at least theoretically) that the more variations in key combinations, the higher the security. Or is it? I believe two-dimensional locks provide greater security. What's the reason for this enigma?

It seems that multiple dimension (round, square, or thick tumblers housed in other objects that must shear) allows for easy dexterity in picking the lock! This is because most humans function in three dimensions (some of us in four dimensions plus, depending on the brew). And some of the new, high-security locks that are based on tumbler variations at different and unique angles to shear line (or latch line) are extremely difficult to pick. But, they *can be opened*.

However, digital-type security systems (two-dimensional formats such as 1 = on, 0 = off—as used in digital electronics, or more basically, up-down/left-right, as used in electronic scanners) have produced the most impregnable security systems devised by man. Picking a three-dimensional lock is easy. Picking a two-dimensional lock can be nearly impossible. Flat-tumbler locks will, in a few decades, rule the new age of modern security. But most—for now—can be opened with dexterity, logic, or "tracking" (see *Modern High-Security Locks* for more information).

BIBLIOGRAPHY

Hampton, Steven. *Advanced Lock Picking Secrets*. Boulder, Colo.: Paladin Press, 1989.

————. *Affordable Security*. Boulder, Colo.: Paladin Press, 2004.

————. *Modern High Security Locks*. Boulder, Colo.: Paladin Press, 2002.

————. *Secrets of Lock Picking*. Boulder, Colo.: Paladin Press, 1987.